Raeburn's Rival

Archibald Skirving 1749–1819

SPONSORED BY

BELL LAWRIE WHITE

RAEBURN'S RIVAL

Archibald Skirving
1749–1819

STEPHEN LLOYD

SCOTTISH NATIONAL PORTRAIT GALLERY
MCMXCIX

Published 1999 by the Trustees of the
National Galleries of Scotland for the exhibition
Raeburn's Rival · Archibald Skirving 1749–1819
held at the Scottish National Portrait Gallery, Edinburgh
from 22 January to 5 April 1999

ISBN 0 903598 92 2

Designed and typeset in ITC Bodoni by Dalrymple
Printed and bound by BAS Printers Ltd

Front cover:
Archibald Skirving *Self-portrait* 1790 [61] detail

Back cover: After Sir Henry Raeburn *Archibald Skirving c.*1810 [155]

Frontispiece: Archibald Skirving
An Unknown Family in Rome, 1792 [76] detail

Bell Lawrie White
is an award winner under the Pairing Scheme
(the National Heritage Arts Sponsorship Scheme)
for its support of this exhibition.

The Pairing Scheme is a Government Scheme
managed by ABSA (Association for Business
Sponsorship of the Arts).

Contents

FOREWORD

Archibald Skirving was one of the finest pastellists of the eight-eenth century, yet, compared with his European and English contemporaries, he is little known. This catalogue has been written to accompany the first exhibition ever to have been held of the work of Skirving and it is a sequel to two recent exhibitions staged by the Scottish National Portrait Gallery. The first was on the work of Allan Ramsay, who retired from painting just before Skirving started up in practice, and the second was on Sir Henry Raeburn, Skirving's slightly younger contemporary.

Archibald Skirving worked in oil, in pencil or chalk and in miniature as well as in pastel, and Dr Stephen Lloyd, an Assist-ant Keeper at the Scottish National Portrait Gallery who has curated this exhibition, has explored each aspect of his art. He has examined the influence on him of his contemporaries, the benefits of his seven-year-long stay in Rome and considered how his eccentric behaviour, much remarked on at the time, may have affected his success and reputation.

Skirving's art – particularly in pastel – has always attracted a discriminating, if small, band of admirers. Sir Walter Scott, for instance, considered him 'an unrivalled artist as a painter in crayons'. Thomas Carlyle wrote of his 'consummate skill in por-traiture'. This exhibition, held during the two hundred and fiftieth anniversary of his birth, allows the present generation a unique opportunity to discover an outstanding talent.

Few exhibitions can be mounted today without the willing-ness of lenders, public and private, to part with their treasures. The National Galleries of Scotland are very grateful to them all, and to Bell Lawrie White who have generously sponsored the exhibition.

TIMOTHY CLIFFORD *Director, National Galleries of Scotland*
JAMES HOLLOWAY *Keeper, Scottish National Portrait Gallery*

Preface and Acknowledgements

An encounter with Archibald Skirving's little-known portraits, chiefly drawn in pastel or crayon, usually elicits a frisson of surprise and pleasure from the viewer. So great is the skill and the sensitivity with which the artist has drawn these Scottish sitters, that at first glance it seems that these expertly drawn pastels are actually painted in oil. On closer examination one can revel in the freshness of the colouring and admire the uncompromising frankness and remarkable lack of sentimentality with which the sitters are portrayed. Their presence is palpable. Such was my reaction in 1993 when invited to mount a small display at the Portrait Gallery of our five pastel and crayon portraits.

All commentators on the history of Scottish art have noted the outstanding quality of Skirving's portraiture in pastels, but he has usually been discussed, if at all, as a postcript to much longer accounts of his younger contemporary, Sir Henry Raeburn (1756–1823). The title 'Raeburn's Rival' is provocative, in that it invites comparison between the two portraitists. Their careers were similar in many respects, with both men starting their careers as miniaturists in Edinburgh; both travelled to Rome in the mid-1780s to further their studies, and they returned to practice professionally in Edinburgh, utterly transformed as artists by their Italian experiences.

Raeburn became the brilliant, prolific portrait painter in oils of Scottish society, while Skirving mastered the difficult, time-consuming, and less fashionable art of painting in crayons. Raeburn, who was socially adept, ran a very busy studio, producing over a thousand oil portraits in his thirty-five-year-long career after his return from Italy. Skirving, on the other hand, who was proud, sly and difficult to befriend, was by all accounts temperamentally unsuited to the necessarily sociable business of portraiture. As a result, and combined with his high prices, numerous sittings and slow completion rate, he undertook only a few portraits during his more than twenty-year-long career after returning from Italy.

The two artists make for interesting comparison. While it is difficult to compare them in terms of style – Raeburn instinctive, impressionistic, visionary, Skirving lucid, graphic and precise in terms of outline and colour – what is in no doubt is their similarity in sheer talent and in the degree of mastery of their craft. Both achieved visual masterpieces in different ways with different effects. In terms of ability and achievement, Skirving and Raeburn are indeed rivals.

Because of Skirving's relatively small output, an exhibition principally devoted to Skirving has never previously taken place. In addition, a number of his key portraits are still in private hands, often descendants of the sitters themselves. Thus, very few portraits by Skirving have come onto the art market. In addition, due to the fragility of pastels, exhibitions of works in this medium are rare. I am especially grateful to all the lenders, but in particular the private owners, for agreeing that their portraits should be lent to this exhibition. These lenders have also been most generous in providing information on their ancestors. Happily, a number of Skirving's works still belong to descendants of the Skirving family, not through the artist himself, who neither married nor had children, but through his siblings, as well as his half-brother and half-sisters.

I am very grateful to the many people who have patiently and generously answered my numerous enquiries or assisted in various ways: Julia Armstrong-Totten, James Berry, Patrick Bourne, Patricia Brassey, Iain Gordon Brown,

Richard Calvocoressi, Michael Clarke, Honor Clerk, Sir John and Lady Clerk of Penicuik, Katherine Coombs, John Dick, Simon Edsor, Alexandra Fennell, Peter Funnell, Graeme Gollan, Ian Gow, Peter Gray, Antony Griffiths, Malcolm Hay, Robin Hodge, Valerie Hunter, John Ingamells, Muriel King, David Lavender, Sue Makin, Ann Macintosh, Peter McEwan, Margaret Mackay, David Mackie, Alexander Meddowes, Anthony Mould, Philip Mould, Jan Newton, Michael Phillips, Nicholas Phillipson, Peter Raissis, Antonia Reeve, Donald A. Reid, Jeremy Rex-Parkes, Linsay Robertson, Charles Saumarez Smith, Sir Robert Shields, Jacob Simon, Murray Simpson, Lydia Skinner, T. Bain Smith, Dianne Stein, Karen Stewart, William Stout, Duncan Thomson, Janette Thomson, Katrina Thomson, Alan and Mary Thompson, Nancy Thorburn, Anne Marie Wagener, Richard Walker, Alasdair White, and William Zachs.

My research on Archibald Skirving has been encouraged and facilitated by many people; inevitably art historians build on the work of predecessors in their field. In particular I am indebted to the late Basil Skinner, a former Assistant Keeper in the Scottish National Portrait Gallery, for his encouragement of my interest in the work of Skirving, and – just before he died – for placing his notes on the artist at my disposal. His pioneering article on Skirving published in the 1970 volume of the *Transactions of the East Lothian Antiquarian and Field Naturalists' Society*, which included a list of all the documented and known works by the artist, is still of the greatest use today. Basil Skinner in turn greatly benefited from being given access to the life-long research on Skirving by Mrs Leila Hoskins, a collateral descendant of the artist. Most generously she presented the pastel of *Gavin Hamilton* [60] to the Portrait Gallery in 1981. Unfortunately, much of the original source material she had collected was inadvertently destroyed after her death two years later. More recently, there has also been an excellent thesis on Skirving, with a catalogue of his work, researched and written by the Swedish art historian, Tanja Sundström.

I am particularly grateful to my colleagues Keith Morrison for his help on frames, Rosalind Marshall for her advice on dress, and Helen Smailes for her knowledge of the early documents. I am also grateful to Robin Hamlyn, Duncan Macmillan and Francis Russell for sharing their specialist knowledge and enthusiasm. Finally, I thank Alice Thompson for devising the challenging title to this exhibition, which will hopefully draw people to rediscover the extraordinary portraiture of Archibald Skirving, this hitherto unjustly obscure Scottish artist, and that, as Basil Skinner hoped, 'a fuller appreciation of his merit be achieved'.

STEPHEN LLOYD *Scottish National Portrait Gallery*

Throughout this publication
numbers shown within square brackets [thus] refer to
the Catalogue numbers.

ARCHIBALD SKIRVING
1749–1819

1 · EAST LOTHIAN, EDINBURGH AND LONDON
1749–1786

In 1818, a year before Skirving's death, Thomas Carlyle [152] saw the artist emerge from a street in Edinburgh on a brilliant summer's morning, 'the sky as bright as diamonds'. Fifty years later the great historian recalled Skirving's appearance on that day:

An altogether striking man. Wiry, elastic, perpendicular, and of good inches, still brisk-looking, tho' perhaps 70 odd; spotlessly clean, his linen white as snow, no necktie but a loosish-fastened black ribbon; hair all grey, not white, nor over-long; face, neck, hands of a fine brown tint; one of the cleanest old men I ever saw; – and such a face as you would still more rarely see. Eagle-like; nose hooked like an eagle's bill, eyes still with something of the eagle's flash in them; squarish prominent brow, under-jaw ditto, cheeks & neck thin, sensitively wrinkled, – brow, cheek, jaws, chin all betokening impetuosity, rapidity, delicacy and the stormy fire of genius not yet hidden under the ashes of old age. A face and figure never to be forgotten.[1]

With these words Carlyle concluded his vivid manuscript memoir, or 'picture' of the artist, which he fancied 'Skirving himself could not beat'.

Archibald Skirving was the elder son of Adam Skirving [42, figs.1–2] by his first wife Jean Ainslie from Haddington. They had married in 1748 and Archibald was born at East Garleton farm the following year. The Skirvings had two other children, Robert [156], who became a captain in the service of the East India Company, and Grace [106], both of whom married members of the Ainslie family. After Jean Ainslie's death, Adam Skirving remarried in 1768, his second wife being Christian Carnegie from North Berwick [fig.3]. They had a son David, who married a Carnegie, and

three daughters, Elizabeth and Janet (or Jessy) [85], both of whom also married members of the Carnegie family, and Magdalene, who married an Ainslie. It was David Skirving, rather than his elder half-brother Archibald, who, after the death of their father in 1803, took over the lease of East Garleton farm. The Skirving family was extremely close-knit and connected by marriage to other local farming families, and a number of the artist's sitters would be drawn from either his own family or those of his neighbours.

Adam Skirving was the tenant at East Garleton farm on the Wemyss estate, which is near the village of Athelstaneford, just north of the county town of Haddington, and about fifteen miles east of Edinburgh [55]. The surrounding countryside is rich agricultural land, mainly used for arable farming. The Skirving family's landlord was the Hon. Francis Charteris of Amisfield, who in 1787 became the 7th Earl of Wemyss [23, 30, fig.4]; his seat of Amisfield was located just to the east of Haddington. The Charteris family were to play an important role in the development of Archibald Skirving as an artist, since they were probably instrumental in supporting his long stay in Italy from 1787 to 1794.

The parish of Athelstaneford was described at some length in 1792 in the *Statistical Account of Scotland*. Just under 700 inhabitants had been recorded in 1755, and there is a note on the remarkable number of 'distinguished characters' produced by the village. Among those briefly mentioned were Robert Blair (1699–1746), who was a minister of the parish and author of the famous poem *The Grave*; his son Robert Blair (1741–1811), Lord President of the College of Justice; the Revd John Home [127], also a minister of the parish and author of what was then the very well-known *Tragedy of Douglas*; and a young artist, whose name is not given, but who must be Archibald Skirving:

Painting, too, the sister art of poetry, has been cultivated here with taste and advantage. The son of a respectable farmer in this parish, from his earliest years discovered a remarkable genius for drawing and painting. As he advanced in life, he applied chiefly to miniatures, in which he excelled. For these several years past, he has been in Italy; and there is good reason to believe that he ranks among the first artists in that country.[2]

Archibald Skirving's father, Adam, was a well-respected farmer in East Lothian, who composed the famous Jacobite ballads, 'Hey, Johnnie Cope' [58] and 'Tranent Muir', about events surrounding the battle of Prestonpans in 1745. As late as 1862, when Samuel Smiles wrote *The Lives of the Engineers*, he recalled Adam Skirving's caustic wit against the commanding officers of the government forces. After the publication of 'Hey, Johnnie Cope' had offended some of Cope's officers, one of them, Lieutenant Smith, sent Skirving a challenge from the George Inn at Haddington. When the messenger arrived, the farmer was in his yard turning over manure. After reading the letter, Skirving said: 'Ye may gang back to Lieutenant Smith, and say to him, if he likes to come up-by here, I'll tak' a look at him; if I've a mind to fecht him, I'll fecht him; and if no, I'll do as he did – I'll rin awa!'[3]

Little is known of Archibald Skirving's early life, but he would have received his education locally. According to the novelist and essayist Henry Mackenzie (1745-1831), who knew Skirving, in his notes on contemporary painters and architects, his father secured his eldest son, on coming of age, a job as a junior clerk in the Customs Office in Edinburgh. The art critic George Cleghorn, who also knew the artist, wrote in his book *Ancient and Modern Art*, first published in 1837, that Skirving's father

accompanied him to Edinburgh, saw him installed in his office, and presenting him with half-a-crown to buy a penknife, intimated to him that he was never to look to him for more – and he kept his word. Skirving left to his own shifts, was obliged to adopt the most rigid economy to live within his very limited means. What originated at first from necessity, became in after life habitual, when he was comparatively rich.[4]

This was the beginning of Skirving's life-long reputation for frugality, and for which he became legendary among his contemporaries. Mackenzie described how at the same time as Skirving continued his day job, even then he

devoted himself to painting, and did several miniatures, in water colours of very considerable merit, among which I recollect two that got him a great deal of reputation, one of his father and one of Lady Eleanor Hume, daughter of Lord Hume, both excellent subjects for a painter. This bringing him to notice, and affording him from the price of several other miniatures some money, which to him, a man of no expense, made in a short time a stock to begin the world with, he used it properly in a journey and some stay at Rome, where he improved himself in his art, which he now confined to painting in crayons, which in one of his singular fancies, he said was the only good mode of painting.[5]

Reconstructing Archibald Skirving's early career as a miniaturist in Edinburgh is particularly difficult as so few of his portraits have survived from that period. The miniature which is clearly a touchstone for these years is the now untraced portrait of the artist's father, Adam Skirving [fig.1], which can be dated to *c*.1770. Painted with extraordinary skill and intense realism, the artist paints his father close-up and directly facing the viewer. There is no attempt at flattery or idealisation, and this would be a notable characteristic of all Skirving's portraiture. Not only was this miniature praised by Henry Mackenzie, but also by Thomas Carlyle, who was shown it in 1832 by the artist's brother, Robert. The historian described it as

by far the best Portrait I had then ever seen of any man; and which I vividly remembered again, 10 years after, on sight of the first real Oliver Cromwell *by* Cooper, *– real, not fictitious & imaginary, as above nine-tenths of them are, – which was vouchsafed me. Nothing so excellent had I ever seen before.*[6]

Very little is known about how Skirving studied as an artist. A clue, however, is provided by an inscription on the reverse of a head and shoulders *Self-portrait* [fig.5], an oil on canvas which probably dates to around 1770. This reads 'Revillon', almost certainly a mistaken reference to Charles Pavillon,

Fig.1: *Adam Skirving c.*1770, by Archibald Skirving
Location Unknown

Fig.2: *Adam Skirving c.*1770, by Archibald Skirving
The Art Gallery of New South Wales, Sydney

Fig.3: *Christian Carnegie, Mrs Adam Skirving c.*1770,
by Archibald Skirving
The Art Gallery of New South Wales, Sydney

Fig.4: *The Hon. Francis Charteris of Amisfield
(later 7th Earl of Wemyss)* 1779, by Richard Cosway [30]
The Rt Hon. the Earl of Wemyss & March, KT

who was Master of the Trustees' Academy in Edinburgh from 1768 to 1772. The Trustees' Academy had been established in 1760 to provide instruction for pupils who were intending to pursue a trade. Formal training was offered, with premiums, for 'the encouragement of arts, sciences, manufactures and agriculture'. The Frenchman William Delacour was the first Master, from 1760 to 1767, followed by Pavillon, also a Frenchman, who had been a drawing master in London. He in turn was followed by Alexander Runciman who had recently returned from Italy [13], from 1772 until his death. Runciman was succeeded by David Allan, who was Master from 1786 until his death in 1796. It is very likely that Skirving was taught how to paint and draw at the Trustees' Academy.[7] This *Self-portrait* is a precocious work for a twenty-year old artist. Skirving gazes intently at himself in the mirror, and out to the viewer, although he is not yet confident enough to include either of his hands in the composition.

In 1770, at about the same date as the *Self-portrait*, Skirving painted three further oil portraits, two versions of a portrait of his father [42, fig.2], and one of his stepmother, Christian Carnegie [fig.3]. These head and shoulder portraits depict the sitters in feigned ovals and are competent in their execution and confident in their characterisation. However, Skirving still does not feel able to include the hands. The portraits of his father are more carefully painted, in particular the incidental details, while in that of his stepmother the paint is more freely handled, notably in the dress.[8]

Only two pastels can be placed – and then tentatively – in Skirving's early period during the 1770s. A rather flatly drawn copy of the head of David Martin's three-quarter length portrait of *Henry Dundas (later 1st Viscount Melville)* [4, fig.6] from 1770 has traditionally been attributed to Skirving, as well as a charming pastel portrait of *An Unknown Girl* [5, fig.7]. While these two early pastels do not match the quality of the work that Skirving produced in Rome, they can be compared to the early oil portraits and can be seen as early indicators of the artist's later concentration on pastel as his favoured medium.

Despite these essays, Skirving clearly was not completely at ease either with oil painting or drawing in crayons and devoted himself to portrait miniatures. It is not known how he was taught to paint in this medium but it is probable that he learned the technique either from another artist or from a goldsmith and jeweller. One can assume that he followed a similar career in this respect to Henry Raeburn [83, 160], who was seven years younger than Skirving. After his education at George Heriot's Hospital in Edinburgh, Raeburn was apprenticed in 1772 for seven years to James Gilliland, a goldsmith and jeweller in Parliament Square. A number of Raeburn's miniatures are known from the 1770s.[9] The most significant is that from 1773 of *David Deuchar* [24], a goldsmith, seal engraver and amateur etcher.

The origins of Raeburn's training as a miniaturist are less obscure than Skirving's, in that it is likely that James Gilliland would either have had a hand in Raeburn's tuition, or encouraged his obvious skill in taking a likeness on the small scale. However, in the search for the source of Skirving's and Raeburn's development as portrait miniaturists in the 1770s, it is possible to speculate that they studied with an as yet unidentified figure in Edinburgh. Certainly, during the previous decade of the 1760s, accomplished and carefully painted miniatures were being painted there in a similar style to that of Skirving and Raeburn [18–20].[10]

There was a sufficiently developed, if limited, market and clientele for miniatures in Edinburgh, to enable two highly talented young artists to choose this specialised medium. Edinburgh was a small capital city but important as a seat of administration and justice, as well as containing inhabitants with considerable intellectual aspirations. By 1772 the planned New Town was being shown on maps, such as Thomas Kitchin's *Plan of the City, Castle and Suburbs of Edinburgh* [52], and was being laid out to the north of the Old Town. Skirving may well have known his contemporary James Craig, the architect who had devised the layout of the New Town, as he owned a small full-length oil portrait of him, ascribed to David Allan [47, fig.8].

After ten years working in the Edinburgh Customs House by day and practising as a miniaturist by night, by late 1777 at the age of twenty-eight Skirving was keen to test his vocation, skill and fortune as a portrait miniaturist in London. It

Fig.5: *Self-portrait c.*1770, by Archibald Skirving
The Art Gallery of New South Wales, Sydney

Fig.6: *Henry Dundas (later 1st Viscount Melville) c.*1770–80,
attributed to Archibald Skirving after David Martin [4]
The Dundas-Bekker Family

Fig.7: *An Unknown Girl c.*1770–80, attributed to
Archibald Skirving [5]
Elisabeth A. McIntyre

Fig.8: *James Craig c.*1780, ascribed to David Allan [47]
Scottish National Portrait Gallery, Edinburgh

is known that he had letters of introduction, one of which was to John Hamilton Mortimer (1741–79), noted for his history paintings and conversation pieces. During this time in London, Skirving exhibited only once at the newly founded Royal Academy. In 1778, described as a 'miniature painter', he displayed 'a frame with three miniatures'. The catalogue listed his address or lodgings as 'at Mrs Milward's, Little Brook Street, Hanover Square'.[11]

To live in the fashionable West End of London was essential for a young artist, but Skirving must have found the competition among the miniaturists fierce. Not only was he competing with other Scottish miniaturists, who had moved to London and were developing successful careers, men such as Charles Shirreff [36], James Scouler [22], John Donaldson [39] and, in particular, John Bogle [21, 32–4], but he also had to compete with established and prolific miniaturists such as Samuel Cotes [25], Richard Crosse, George Engleheart [29], Ozias Humphry [23], Jeremiah Meyer, John Smart and, most prominently, the fashionable and self-publicising Richard Cosway [30, 38, fig.4].[12]

Intriguingly, Skirving attempted to follow the fashion set by Richard Cosway – as, for example, in the latter's engagingly direct portraits of Charles Anderson-Pelham, later 1st Baron Yarborough, and of his son Charles of c.1785 [38]. Skirving adopted a light palette and white cloudy background, which is shot through with blue sky. The works by Skirving that have been identified from this period are the signed and dated *Unknown Lady*

[fig.9] of 1780, the sitter shown holding a piece of paper;[13] the similar *An Unknown Lady* [31], where the lady holds a mask and *Anne Biddulph, Mrs Gordon* [35] from c.1785. In the light of Skirving's blunt portrayal of his father in miniature of c.1770 [fig.1], and from what is known of his character, one might have expected him to follow a more realistic approach in his portrayal of the sitters in these miniatures, following the example of John Bogle, George Engleheart and John Smart.

Skirving must have found it difficult to make his mark in London, as by the mid-1780s he had returned to Edinburgh. It is known from a letter that he was working on portraits of Miss Hume of Ninewells, John Hume and Mrs Lockhart. He also had problems with his eyesight and with his health. His younger brother, Robert, wrote to the artist on 9 August 1786:

Now that you have determined to settle back in Edinburgh, I hope you will find yourself much more at ease ... I'm very glad you paint only in crayons as it will not be so bad for your eyes nor confine your chest so much; and I remember yon picture you did at Dunbar that pleased me exceedingly. If you chance to do the heads of my acquaintances, instead of rubbing them out, send them to me.[14]

Skirving's lack of success in London was repeated in Edinburgh. In a letter to his brother that had probably crossed with the one previously quoted from, the artist stated bluntly that 'I have resolved to finish my career in Edinburgh to prevent the public doing it for me.'[15]

Fig.9: *An Unknown Lady* 1780, by Archibald Skirving
Victoria & Albert Museum, London

By 1786 Skirving had decided to pursue his artistic studies and develop his skill in Italy, principally in Rome. This was a traditional destination for many British artists during the eighteenth century. Among the most prominent Scots to make the journey were Allan Ramsay [2], Gavin Hamilton [7, 60, 79], Alexander Runciman [13], Jacob More [78], Richard Cooper, David Allan, John Runciman [41], John Brown and Henry Raeburn [83].[16]

Skirving left Leith by boat on 30 November 1786. He was to remain in Italy for nearly seven and a half years. By all accounts he had saved some money over the years from his modest portrait practice. However, as with other artists travelling to Rome, it is very likely that he would have had financial support from an interested benefactor. Skirving appears to have been assisted by the Charteris family, either the Hon. Francis Charteris of Amisfield [23, 30, fig.4], or his only son Viscount Elcho [62]. In late 1789 Lord Elcho made a six-month visit to Italy with his wife and two of his children. They visited Skirving, who was by then established in Rome, and both father and son sat for their portraits in pastels. In a letter from Lord Elcho to Robert Skirving, written from Rome on 6 January 1790, he noted:

I am happy to inform you that your brother has acquired one of the first characters here for merit in his profession and for his general conduct. I hope to have it in my power to be of great use to him in making his talents known, and – when they are – they cannot fail to be esteemed.[17]

In Rome Skirving took lodgings in the parish of S. Maria del Popolo. He soon found himself part of the colony of artists. Three years later he was noted – in a list of twenty-one British painters and sculptors in Rome – as staying in the Palazzo Babuino in the artists' quarter near the Piazza di Spagna, where he had established himself as 'a portraitist in crayons'. His name also appears in a letter of 1794 from twenty-three British artists in Rome, thanking Prince Augustus, a younger son of George III, for obtaining help to waive the payment of duties on their artworks when being imported back into Britain. From Skirving's correspondence with the London art critic George Cumberland, towards the end of his stay in Rome in 1794, it is clear that he had made close contacts with a number of artists in Rome, such as Jacob More [78], and the sculptor Henry Deare. It is also known from Mrs Flaxman's diary that in 1791 Skirving had started work on a portrait of her husband, the sculptor John Flaxman (untraced).[18]

Skirving was also familiar with foreign artists, such as the German portraitist Johann Heinrich Wilhelm Tischbein and the Italian landscapist and watercolour painter G.B. Lusieri, both working in Naples in 1793, to whom he provided letters of introduction for the Scottish banker Sir William Forbes [82]. Forbes visited Rome in 1792 and 1793, together with his wife and daughter, and referred to Skirving on a number of occasions in his manuscript journal, once calling him 'a very ingenious' artist. On 30 April 1793 Forbes described the artist as follows: 'Skirving, another old acquaintance from Edinburgh, paints small portraits with considerable merit but he takes so much time and bestows so much labour in finishing his pieces that he can never do much – indeed can scarcely live by his art.'[19]

Within a year of his arrival in Rome, Skirving was working as an agent for, and receiving commissions from, the wealthy retired judge Francis Garden, Lord Gardenstone, who visited Italy in 1787–8 as part of a wider Grand Tour – Gardenstone's *Travelling Memorandums* was first published in 1791, two years before his death. Lord Gardenstone particularly admired certain artists resident in Rome: Angelica Kauffman, Gavin Hamilton and Jacob More. One of Lord Gardenstone's main pleasures in Italy was to 'search for articles for my Cabinet of Natural History', which was comprised of precious stones, as well as cameos, coins and small paintings. While in Rome during February and March 1788, he bought – for 45 sequins – two small copies by Skirving 'of Correggio's admired picture of the Gamesters, the original in the palace of Fidmar', as well as 'The Gipsy' by the same artist (in fact Caravaggio). Gardenstone also contracted Skirving, whom he described as 'a young painter of merit …

from the neighbourhood of Edinburgh', to undertake various activities:

> He takes charge of those paintings and my collection of Natural History, to have all shipped for London; and I have given him in writing commissions as follows:
>
> 1. To draw a miniature painting for me of the worthy and ingenious painter Mr Gavin Hamilton.
>
> 2. To try if he can purchase for me some specimens of the cameos made on incrustations.
>
> 3. Also specimens and choice pieces of alum from the mines of Tosta.[20]

The whereabouts of the miniature of Gavin Hamilton is not known, but its appearance can be visualised from a powerful pastel that must have been drawn around the same date [60]. Skirving presented Hamilton, almost in profile, strongly lit, and with a memorable contrast of blue cloak and white turban set against a neutral background. This arresting image could not be in greater contrast to Ozias Humphry's more conventional portrait drawing of Hamilton made in Rome over a decade earlier, in 1777 [7].

Some of Skirving's other activities in Rome were detailed in a letter of 18 December 1790, which he sent to his brother Robert, then in India, in which he referred to some of his portrait commissions and an extended visit to Naples:

> I told you I had painted Lord Elcho's portrait. I did afterwards his cousin called Gordon, a Mr Cleghorn from St Andrew's, Sir John Macpherson's for Mr McAuley, a copy whereof I have to make for poet Home ... I have likewise done another India gentleman ... was an architect. I went to Naples the 6 July last where I remained five months and had the fortune to see a considerable eruption of Vesuvius. I made a copy in Crayon of a picture in the possession of the Minister – Sir William Hamilton K.T. – and expect it daily to arrive.[21]

Of the portraits listed here, the only one that has survived or been identified apart from that of *Francis Charteris, Viscount Elcho* [62], is the pastel of *Hugh Cleghorn of Stravithie* [64, fig.10], professor of history at St Andrews University, who acted as bear-leader or guide to Alexander Home, 10th Earl of Home [65, fig.11], during their six-month visit to Italy from late 1789. Skirving probably made his unidentified

'copy in Crayon' from one of the Old Master paintings in the famous collection of the British envoy, Sir William Hamilton. It is likely that Hamilton, hearing of Skirving's growing reputation in Rome, invited him to Naples and commissioned him to draw a portrait of himself. This untraced portrait, probably in pastel, which showed Hamilton in his dressing-gown and night-cap, was such a success that Hamilton paid Skirving the extraordinarily generous sum of 200 guineas.[22]

Skirving also drew a number of other life-size head and shoulder pastel portraits in Rome. Three of these portraits were documented in the possession of Patrick Murray of Simprim – the illegitimate son of the 5th Baron Elibank – when he was in Rome in 1791, accompanied by his tutor, the Revd Daniel Robertson, professor of Hebrew at the University of St Andrews.[23] Two of the three portraits represented Murray and his tutor, while the other was described as a *Self-portrait* [61]. With its confident pose, assured drawing and emphatic colouring, this striking work represents a remarkable achievement by an artist who had hitherto only enjoyed limited success, whether in Edinburgh or London. Most notable is the prominence given by Skirving in the composition to the black beaver hat, which daringly shadows the artist's brow and eyes. This formal device had been used over twenty years earlier in an oil *Self-portrait* [41] by John Runciman. After the latter's premature death in 1768, his self-portrait probably came into the possession of his brother. As Alexander Runciman [13] returned to Scotland from Rome in 1771, it is likely that Skirving would have known this self-portrait. The device of a wide-brimmed hat to cast a shadow across the brow and eyes was also used by Raeburn, especially in a number of the portraits he painted after his return from Italy in 1786. It is noteworthy that both Skirving and Raeburn were using this unusual and daring lighting device in their portraits simultaneously, yet apparently without any knowledge of the other's work in Edinburgh or Rome.[24]

The careers of Skirving and Raeburn continued to parallel each other to a certain extent at this period, although there were a number of differences. Both of them had started out as miniaturists in Edinburgh, but Raeburn, unlike Skirving, had not attempted to set himself up as an artist in

Fig.10: *Hugh Cleghorn of Stravithie* 1790,
by Archibald Skirving [64]
Private Collection

Fig.11: *Alexander Home, 10th Earl of Home* 1790,
by Hugh Douglas Hamilton [65]
The Rt Hon. the Earl of Home CVO, CBE

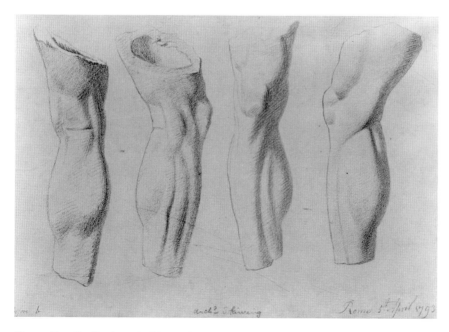

Fig.12: *Four Studies from the Plaster Cast of a Leg* 1793,
by Archibald Skirving [77]
National Gallery of Scotland, Edinburgh

Fig.13: *An Entrance to a Park c.*1787–94,
by Archibald Skirving [68]
National Gallery of Scotland, Edinburgh

Fig.14: *Father James McCormick c.*1787–94,
by Archibald Skirving [66]
Andrew Skirving

Fig.15: *An Unknown Gentleman* 1793,
by Archibald Skirving
Location Unknown

London. It is likely that Raeburn had assisted David Martin, the leading portrait painter resident in Edinburgh after the retirement of Allan Ramsay in the mid-1770s. Raeburn was describing himself as a 'Portrait Painter in Edinburgh' by 1784, and this suggests that he was painting oil portraits before he visited Rome. However, because of the scarcity of works from this period, it is difficult to map out Raeburn's career before he went to Italy. The rather schematically painted three-quarter length portrait of a *Lady in a Lace Cap* has been plausibly attributed to Raeburn and dated to the early 1780s.

Only two portraits can be securely dated from Raeburn's visit to Rome from 1784 to 1786: the sensitive head and shoulders oil portrait of Patrick Moir shown reading and almost in profile, and the confidently painted miniature in oil of *George John Spencer, 2nd Earl Spencer* [37], which was copied from an untraced portrait in crayons by Hugh Douglas Hamilton. The few works that Raeburn produced during his relatively short visit to Rome indicate that he had not yet found his mature style. However, once he had returned to Scotland, he immediately put into practice everything he had assimilated during the Italian visit. By contrast, after a few years in Rome, Skirving had quickly developed his pastel technique to produce such confident early masterpieces as the *Self-portrait* [61] and *Gavin Hamilton* [60].

Skirving, like Raeburn, transformed his ability as a portraitist in Rome, through his exposure to Italian art and training. Both artists would also have had access to a number of studios belonging to artists from Italy and from across Europe. The portraits created by Skirving in Rome have a strong, simple neo-classical appearance, and it may be conjectured that he would have known the modern style of Jacques-Louis David, through one of his main pupils in Rome, Baron François-Xavier Fabre (1766–1837), resident there from 1787 to 1793. Skirving would have improved his pastel technique, most probably by studying with the finest pastellist in the city, the Irishman Hugh Douglas Hamilton, who was resident in Rome from 1782 to 1791. There are strong parallels between the work of the two artists, who both used clear lighting, strong colour and expert draughtsmanship. It is instructive to compare Skirving's pastels drawn in Rome to Hamilton's portraits from this period, such as the pair of oils of *Prince Charles Edward Stewart* [49] in old age and his daughter *The Duchess of Albany* [50], both painted just after 1785. Skirving's work is even closer in style to the pastels of Hamilton, as in the Irish artist's masterpiece, *Antonio Canova in his Studio with Hugh Tresham*, drawn in 1788–9, and a more typical portrait head, such as *Alexander Home, 10th Earl of Home* [65, fig.11], dated 1790.[25]

Like many foreign artists resident in Rome, Skirving may have studied in one of the art schools, possibly the French Academy. There is the evidence of an academy drawing in red and black chalks by Skirving, dated 5 April 1793, which shows four studies from the plaster cast of a leg [77, fig.12]. Skirving also honed his skill as a draughtsman, by making 'en plein air' landscape drawings across Rome. These sensitive studies in red and black chalks or pencil show a variety of views both formal and informal, whether looking through a park to sculptures, as in *An Entrance to a Park* [68, fig.13], or *The Fontana dei Cavalli Marini in the Borghese Gardens* [75],[26] or various studies of buildings that include *The Dome of St Peter's Basilica* [71]. Less formal, though no less carefully observed, are drawings such as *A Landscape with Three Stags* [67], *Donkey and Foal* [69] and *A Canopy Suspended from a Tree* [70].

The artist also made a few portrait drawings during his visit to Rome. These include the study of *Father James McCormick* [66, fig.14], and the untraced profile portrait drawing of *An Unknown Gentleman* [fig.15] dated 1793. The latter drawing is the first existing example of a type of profile which Skirving produced in considerable numbers on his return to Scotland. The outstanding portrait drawing from the Roman period is the study of *An Unknown Family in Rome* [76, frontispiece], which is signed and dated 1792. Almost certainly representing a Scottish family on the Grand Tour, Skirving shows the father standing in profile and admiring an unseen statue or a building, while drawing with a *porte-crayon* in a sketchbook. Also in profile and turned towards him, is his wife, shown seated on a grassy bank, and staring impassively past her husband. Between the two adults the artist has represented their son, aged about ten, who gazes out directly at the artist and the viewer. The clear drawing and intimate composition of the group, isolated from their surroundings, has invited comparison with the later portrait drawings by Ingres of visitors to Rome.[27]

The cataclysmic impact of the outbreak of the French Revolution in 1789 contributed over the next few years to a substantial reduction in the numbers of British visitors to Italy, and a consequent decline in the Roman art market. These events would have had an impact on Skirving's situation, and deciding to return to Scotland, he left Rome on 22 May 1794. With Britain and France at war, his ship, which had left the Tuscan port of Livorno (Leghorn), was captured by the French off the Straits of Gibraltar on 4 August. Skirving was taken prisoner as a suspected spy, probably on account of the drawing implements and portfolios of sketches he had with him. He was imprisoned in Brest for nine months during the Terror. His health suffered badly and the imprisonment aggravated his eye condition. Nonetheless, he appears to have drawn portraits of officers in the garrison.[28] In a letter of 1802 to his brother Skirving referred to the problems with his eyesight:

> *What I meant of my sight was, that both eyes were equally strong, for you remember I complained of the right one, but small objects appear forked. At Brest after getting out of prison my companion who would buy some pins at the gate remarked that they were all split; he never dreamed the defect was in his sight, and I cannot make a pen tolerable. Glasses would remedy this but they do not well to paint, for painting requires to see different distances.*[29]

News of Skirving's arrest reached the American painter James Smith in Venice on 15 September 1794. In a letter (signed also by Jean-Bernard Duvivier) to Cacault, the French republican *chargé d'affaires* in Florence, he petitioned him for Skirving's release. They stated: 'It would appear to us, both for justice's sake and for the right of being known in France, that the name Shirvin [sic], born in Scotland, who was captured on the same boat, has suffered and suffers still, because of the English tyranny, an atrocious persecution for the sake of liberty. In Rome this artist always showed us the greatest love for the French Revolution.'

The following day Cacault wrote to a colleague about Skirving and a fellow captive, the Flemish sculptor De War: 'I have provided you with an account of the period of imprisonment in the castle of the Holy Angel of citizen de War, a Flemish sculptor … he was captured at sea … the Scottish painter taken with him would also appear to merit some consideration, following the testimony that our patriots have given about his character and his love for our revolution'.[30] After these recommendations, Skirving was released in March 1795, perhaps through an exchange of prisoners. If he travelled home through Paris, he may well have met the great neo-classical artist Jacques-Louis David, who had been profoundly involved in the French Revolution and Terror. Samuel Smiles – in his *The Lives of the Engineers* (1862) – has left the tantalising comment that Skirving 'subsequently studied painting under David'.[31] If Skirving had passed through Paris in order to meet David, it would have to have been before 29 May 1795, when the Revolutionary French painter underwent a second spell in prison – for two months – at the Collège des Quatre-Nations in Paris. Skirving returned to Portsmouth in the summer of 1795.

The experience of imprisonment was said to have badly damaged Skirving's state of mind. In later life Carlyle wrote that the artist lived 'in a secluded, almost *mythic* condition; refusing all work except upon his own whims, and carelessly said by the public to be "cracked" in brain'. Carlyle reluctantly agreed with this opinion. However, the historian put this perception of Skirving's eccentricity and anti-social nature down to the artist's unfortunate experiences in France:

> *In his young days he had gone to Italy enthusiastic for Art-Culture; had fallen among Napoleon's soldierings, been seized as a spy, narrowly missed being shot at once; had then lain long in damp dungeons, in constant danger of his life; and, before deliverance could come, had got his nerves incurably exasperated; a condition which the contradictions of the world, on his return, especially which the shortcomings and obliquities of mankind, inexpressibly detestable to Skirving, had made worse instead of better, and fixed into permanency in the indignant man.*[32]

3 · EDINBURGH, LONDON AND EAST LOTHIAN
1795–1819

After spending a short time in London, Skirving set out north, reaching Berwick-upon-Tweed on 12 August 1795. The ordeal of the imprisonment in France may have affected his eyesight and health, but had not impaired his artistic skill, whether producing pastels, drawings or miniatures. The following decade saw Skirving re-established in Edinburgh, purchasing a flat at 3 St James's Square, on the south side. He also rented an unpretentious two-room studio nearby, at 12 Leith Street or Terrace – unusually, without a show-room or gallery.[33] Skirving had a small portrait practice, preferring to draw those he knew. His attitude to polite society was robust and uncompromising, once stating that 'it is the humour of the people not to employ me because my lodgings are not expensive enough', and also that 'this gives disgust to many who think I should take expensive lodgings for their entertainment'.[34] Thomas Carlyle observed in his posthumous memoir of the artist:

> *For perhaps the last 20 or 15 years of his life, he lived in some* Flat *or* Lodging *all his own (I think, in what was called 'The Terrace', at the head of Leith Walk), in complete Hermitage; an indignant but uncomplaining King, supreme sovereign there if nowhere else. He had some peculium of funds which sufficed him; by temperance and exercise he kept himself in perfect health. Some few, the chosen of the world, he warmly loved; to the multitudinous vulgar, titled and untitled, rich or not rich, he had long since waved his stern* apage *[be gone], and was not concerned with them farther.*[35]

It was there over the next eight years that Skirving created most of the finest work of his career, including such masterpieces in pastel as the tight-lipped and beady-eyed judge, *William Craig, Lord Craig* [89], which can be set against the plain simplicity of the portrait of the artist's half-sister *Janet Skirving, Mrs James Carnegie of Edrom Newton* [85], and the rich textures in the portrait of the lawyer, *Robert Boswell of St Boswells* [84]. The velvety tones of the pastel of *Mary Drummond, Mrs John Pringle of Stitchell* [86] (after an untraced portrait by Danloux) contrast with those in the portrait of the self-confident adolescent, *Henry Home Drummond, 6th Laird of Blair Drummond* [87]. The portrait of *Mrs Johnston of Hutton Hall* [88] has an unusual, highly-keyed exuberance, which contrasts with the profoundly sensitive and reflective *Margaret Sym, Mrs John Wilson* [90]. Other masterpieces from this period include the portrait of the judge, *Alexander Fraser Tytler, Lord Woodhouselee* [91], which is frank and immediate, the characterful portrait of the grizzled *John Clerk of Eldin* [92] and the austere and moving depiction of *An Unknown Lady* [99]. In quite a different mood from these is the charming, and unique, full-length study of *Robert Dundas of Arniston* [95], shown as a child holding an owl. Again, there are a pair of pastels, subtle and restrained, of an elderly couple, the baxter (baker) *Benjamin Yule* and his wife *Marion Sprot* [93-4, figs.16-17], which can be compared with the quite different, romantic vein of the unfinished pastels of *Lady Charlotte Campbell* [98, fig.18] and *Maria Cuninghame of Lainshaw* [100, fig.19]. All of these portraits are marked by an extraordinarily clear and humane vision: simple and sober. The concentration is absolute, and nothing is allowed to interrupt the intense focus by the artist on the sitter.

Skirving's blunt approach to his sitters was criticised by Patrick Gibson (*c.*1782-1829) a younger artist and critic. In the *Edinburgh Annual Register* of 1816, he wrote about Skirving's 'bad taste' in 'placing in the most conspicuous point of view the personal deformities of his subjects, which he most carefully and accurately represented, without regard to the feelings of the individual'. Gibson continued by observing how Skirving offended social practice and etiquette, normally respected by portraitists:

> *It may here appear not a little surprising, that in disregarding the first and great maxim of portrait painting, viz. to make every one well pleased with himself, he should have at all obtained the suffrages of the public in his favour. This might partly have arisen from the acknowledged fidelity with which he represented everything he attempted, as well as from his address in*

Fig.16: *Benjamin Yule c.1796–1800*,
by Archibald Skirving [93]
Private Collection

Fig.17: *Marion Sprot, Mrs Benjamin Yule c.1796–1800*,
by Archibald Skirving [94]
Private Collection

Fig.18: *Lady Charlotte Campbell c.*1802,
by Archibald Skirving [98]
The Fine Art Society, London

Fig.19: *Maria Cuninghame of Lainshaw (later
Maria Cuninghame-Cranstoun of Corehouse) c.*1800–5,
by Archibald Skirving and an Unknown Artist [100]
Private Collection

impressing the public with the idea, that he was confer-
ring a favour on his sitters in accepting their employ-
ment.[36]

Despite having an intense dislike for the eccentric Skirving, the writer Henry Mackenzie, who described the artist on one of his visits to Edinburgh as 'the same rude dogmatical being as ever', wrote a highly revealing account of Skirving's single-minded approach to his working practice as a portraitist:

Time, indeed, he did not well appreciate to himself or
others; and being the most elaborate and minute of
artists made his patients (as they might be called) who
were sitting to him sometimes give him fifty or sixty
sittings. His portraits were facsimiles, *even of the*
blemishes of the faces which he painted; he never spared
a freckle or a smallpox mark, and once, with his charac-
teristic rudeness, told a lady who had a very dingy
complexion he could not paint her, for he had not enough
of yellow chalk for the purpose.[37]

In his anecdotal account of Raeburn's life and career, Mackenzie noted that Raeburn was much superior to Skirving as an artist and more estimable as a man. Likewise, George Cleghorn described Skirving in comparison with Raeburn, making the point that they were different artists in 'style and manner', and that Skirving could not have been said to be a rival to Raeburn, within the professional terms of attracting clients for their respective portrait practices. Yet Cleghorn concedes that Skirving was able to attract a clientele 'of the first rank and eminence in Scotland'.[38] While the two artists created portraits in different mediums, Skirving, at his best, in aesthetic terms, could rival – and at times outdo – the achievements of the younger artist. This was partly due to the fact that the overall quality of Raeburn's work suffered because of the intense demand for his portraiture. In contrast, because Skirving produced relatively few portraits he was able to sustain the high quality of his pastel portraits. The differences between the two artists can be seen most clearly in their interpretations of Alexander Fraser Tytler, Lord Woodhouselee. Skirving's pastel of 1798 shows the sitter clearly lit and with searching frankness [91], while Raeburn's oil of six years later [142, fig.20] is a far more schematically painted work. The differing kinds of sophisti-

cation of both portraits show how far Scottish portrait painting had travelled in two decades, if they are compared, for example, to the earlier oil portrait, attributed to David Allan, of the same sitter shown seated in the library of his father's house at Woodhouselee [46, fig.21].[39]

Skirving's uncompromising attitude to painting the faces of his sitters, 'warts and all', extended to his actual treatment of those who sat to him. George Cleghorn left a fascinating, and seemingly first-hand, account of Skirving's studio and exacting working practice. As the artist did not have a conventional gallery or show-room, anyone who wanted to see his works had to make an appointment, and the time was fixed to the minute. Latecomers were not admitted. On one occasion the Duke of Buccleuch received a rude reception from the artist. Not surprisingly, the artist did not receive a commission from this eminent member of the Scottish nobility. Once admission had been gained and the terms for a portrait agreed, the sitter was always drawn at eye level, 'without any attempt at ideality, or bold effects of light and shadow'. This latter element was in direct contrast to Raeburn's practice.

Skirving's aim in his portraiture appeared to have been verisimilitude. Cleghorn remarked: 'His object was resemblance, character, and a faithful imitation of nature. He never touched the picture, not even the drapery, except in presence of the sitter. Though the details were scrupulously expressed, there was no hardness. He had a perfect knowledge of light and shade.' Cleghorn went on to convey something of the demanding nature of the more than usual number of sittings that were needed by Skirving, whom he described as 'anxious and fastidious in the extreme'. In noting the artist's severe dislike of any interruptions, and his aversion to visitors being present during a sitting, the critic described a notoriously unfinished commission from the eminent society beauty, Lady Charlotte Campbell [98, fig.18], younger sister of George, 6th Duke of Argyll, who was attended by her husband Colonel John Campbell of Shawfield and her pet dog:

Mr Skirving bore with this for a few sittings; at last,
losing all patience, he said to her ladyship at the conclu-
sion of the sitting, 'Lady Charlotte, if you wish me to

complete your portrait, I beg you will leave your husband and lap-dog at home'. This, of course, gave offence, and Lady Charlotte never returned. After the lapse of many years, one of her family applied to Mr Skirving for the portrait, unfinished as it was, and offered to give any price he chose to ask. This, however, he positively refused, as he thought he had been ill treated. [40]

Every contemporary commentator on Skirving referred to his eccentricity, in particular his frugality, but also to his proud and prickly nature. Stories about his unusual behaviour were widespread. Allan Cunningham, the Scottish art critic based in London, described him as 'an eccentric man, who desired to be thought singular, and aspired to be a wit and an epigrammatist'. [41] Moreover, Henry Mackenzie lamented that Skirving 'unluckily took singularity for genius', adding that 'it was impossible to befriend him, because favours he often conceived to be affronts, and valued himself on a proud independence of the world'. [42] Patrick Gibson commented in 1816 that Skirving's 'works are not numerous, as his enthusiasm and genius were equally divided between painting, darning stockings, turning egg-cups, mending his old clothes, and other useful offices'. [43]

Another influential contemporary who recognised Skirving's exceptional talent and skill as a portraitist was the antiquarian, David Steuart Erskine, 11th Earl of Buchan [11], who, in a letter to the Hon. Gilbert Elliot, probably dating from 1809, described a dinner party he had held in Edinburgh for various artists on 10 April that year. Among the guests were John Henning and Skirving, whom he described thus: 'Skervin [*sic*] is a man of faculty & genius but shy, & I have not been able to draw him out by benefits, (tho' penurious), or otherwise. He is much inclined to be a great man'. [44]

Apart from drawing portraits in pastels, Skirving also continued to produce portraits in oil and miniatures. Only two oil portraits can be dated from the period after his return from Italy, and more specifically to around 1800. One of these is of the noted divine and pamphleteer, *The Revd Alexander Carlyle* [143], who was for many years minister at Inveresk, near Musselburgh. The other is the portrait of *An Unknown Gentleman* [144] in old age, which bears a strong resemblance to the artist's father, Adam, especially when

compared to the earlier oils [42, fig.2] and miniature [fig.1]. While these two portraits are expressive and well painted, they do not have the particular force of the pastels, being too dependent on the example of Raeburn's colouring and *chiaroscuro* lighting effects. Observing these competent but unexceptional oil portraits, it is not surprising that Skirving concentrated on pastels and drawings.

With regard to any other stylistic influence on Skirving's portraiture, in particular the pastels, it seems likely that he may have responded to the work of the French *émigré* portraitist, Henri-Pierre Danloux. An ardent monarchist, Danloux was exiled in Britain during the French Revolution, and was based with his family in London for a decade from 1792. He made a number of extended visits to Edinburgh in the years following 1796. There he undertook a number of portraits of members of the exiled French royal family, who had taken refuge in the Palace of Holyroodhouse. Additionally, he painted various eminent Scottish sitters, including Lord Adam Gordon [141], Governor of Edinburgh Castle and Commander of Forces in North Britain; the naval heroes and admirals, Viscount Duncan and Viscount Keith [138, fig.22]; and members of the family of Henry, 3rd Duke of Buccleuch [139]. While it appears that some of the oil sketches were done from *ad vivum* sittings in Edinburgh, the fully worked up oil paintings were executed in Danloux's London studio. [45]

Despite the different mediums used by Skirving and Danloux, there are a number of similarities within the works they created during the second half of the 1790s. Unlike Raeburn, neither artist was particularly interested in the effects of strong shadow or of sitters lit dramatically against dark backgrounds. However, some of Raeburn's paintings from the 1790s, such as *The Revd Robert Walker ('The Skating Minister')*, datable to the middle of that decade, do betray a close awareness of Danloux's striking theatricality. Raeburn may also have been aware of Skirving's and Danloux's simple placement of the sitter against a plain background, as in his *Isabella Macleod, Mrs James Gregory*, painted around 1798. [46]

Skirving's likely contact with Danloux may have involved him in portraying the French artist in a miniature, now

Fig.20: *Alexander Fraser Tytler, Lord Woodhouselee*
1804, by Sir Henry Raeburn [142]
Private Collection

Fig.21: *Alexander Fraser Tytler, Lord Woodhouselee*
1778, attributed to David Allan [46]
Private Collection

Fig.22: *Admiral Sir George Keith Elphinstone*
(later Viscount Keith) 1795-7, by Henri-Pierre Danloux [138]
Private Collection

Fig.23: *Professor James Robertson c.1795-1800,*
by Archibald Skirving after James Tassie
Location Unknown

untraced, but dating to between 1796 and 1800.[47] This portrait is similar to a signed and dated miniature of *An Unknown Gentleman* from 1798 [122]. The confident colouring, light sky background, diagonal cross-hatched brushwork and the forceful characterisation link these two portraits to a number of other miniatures from this date. These include the portrait of *Charles Philippe, Comte d'Artois (later Charles X)* [121] set onto the lid of a snuffbox; *James Drummond, Lord Perth* [124] and his daughter *The Hon. Clementina Sarah Drummond (later Baroness Willoughby de Eresby)* [125].

These rare miniatures can be contrasted with the work of some of Skirving's contemporaries, very few of whom, however, remained in Scotland. One who did was Alexander Gallaway, who produced remarkably unflattering miniatures of his sitters [129]. Most of the talented Scottish miniaturists found work in London, and among those who made successful careers there were Andrew Robertson [128, 131, 133], George Saunders [134], his niece Christina Robertson [135] and Sir William Charles Ross [136]. They all tended to produce more opaquely painted miniatures, that were usually rectangular in format, and which imitated the richness of contemporary oil painting.

Apart from pastels, with the occasional oil or miniature, Skirving's main output consisted of profile portrait drawings, mainly executed in red or black chalk. He had already started these in Rome, in such portraits as *An Unknown Family in Rome* [76, frontispiece], *Father James McCormick* [66] and the *Unknown Gentleman* of 1793 [fig.15], which is untraced. After his return to Edinburgh he produced some outstanding profile portraits, such as *An Unknown Gentleman* of 1797 [104] with its sensitive stippling in red chalk. He also made a delicate pencil copy of a glass paste medallion by James Tassie [151] of *Professor James Robertson* [fig.23], also untraced. In contrast is the simple and informal study of *Patrick Sheriff of Mungoswells* [101, fig.24], a neighbour of the Skirving family at East Garleton, who is shown seated in profile and holding a whip. The artist also made a number of portraits of this type during his visit to London in 1816, such as the *A. Handasyde Esq* [116] and *An Unknown Lady* [117], both in red chalk, with the latter still in its original frame.

Interestingly, it appears that Skirving finished a profile portrait drawing of the noted Edinburgh philosopher, *Professor Dugald Stewart* [115], which had been started by John Henning.

These profile portraits were commented on by Skirving's contemporaries. In her diary entry on 23 July 1802, Jessy Allan, Mrs John Harden (1776-1837), noted a visit to her family household by the artist, who was planning to portray her husband - and amateur draughtsman - John Harden (1772-1847): 'Skirving breakfasted with us & amused us by drawing our profiles with chalk on boards being in very good humor [*sic*]'. Only one such profile on panel is known to exist, that of *The Hon. Charles Napier of Merchiston* [110, fig.25]. However, by contrast, seven years later, in October 1809, when the artist visited the family again, Jessy Harden noted that Skirving was 'an odd Fish & not in my opinion over agreeable'.[48] George Cleghorn also commented on Skirving's more conventional profile portrait drawings [106-9, 112-13, 116-17]: 'He executed occasionally portraits, the size of life, in black chalk - finished in the most delicate manner, and so true to nature, that a sculptor might have modelled from them. Of this description was a portrait of the elder Rennie, the eminent engineer' [159, 162, fig.26].[49]

In the later part of his career it seems that Skirving further reduced his already limited output of portraiture. However, his Edinburgh framers, William Chalmers & Son, were kept engaged with relatively minor work over the period 1814-18, as their bill to the artist attests, totalling just over £20 [167]. Work was done to the 'keel' portrait of Burns in 1814 and a packing box was made in late May 1816, which is evidence for the artist's taking this portrait to London that year. However, there was very little work done in 1817, while in the following year a drawing by the artist of Lady W. Nicolson was 'pasted', presumably onto a backing board. In the same year a frame was ordered for the oil portrait by Andrew Geddes of the artist's brother Robert [156].

Skirving's framing firm of William Chalmers & Son was based at 118 High Street, and was one of a number of such firms with high quality craftsmen based in Edinburgh at this period. Not only did the artist frequent them for such services as frames, glazing, backboards, packing and shipping,

Fig.24: *Patrick Sheriff of Mungoswells* c.1796–1800,
by Archibald Skirving [101]
National Gallery of Scotland, Edinburgh

Fig.25: *The Hon. Charles Napier of Merchiston* 1800
by Archibald Skirving [110]
Glasgow Museums: Art Gallery & Museum, Kelvingrove

Fig.26: *John Rennie* c.1821–2, by E. Scriven
after Archibald Skirving [159]
National Portrait Gallery, London

Fig.27: *Archibald Skirving* c.1810,
by Sir Henry Raeburn
Private Collection, USA

but he also rented accommodation from the firm. In a list of Skirving's debts remaining after his death in 1819, he owed them £29 'house rent'. The artist's careful choice of frames for his works was not only for the typical and handsome carved and gilded profile, but also for the more simple veneered frame made out of woods such as oak, mahogany, walnut and yew. Some of these had a gilded inner slip to help differentiate the picture and the frame [156].

Later in life Skirving appears to have taken up the tutoring of art. There is a family tradition that he taught drawing to the daughters of Francis Charteris, the 8th Earl of Wemyss [63]. In 1862 Samuel Smiles related the anecdote about these lessons to illustrate Skirving's eccentric and sarcastic wit:

> He was at the Earl of Wemyss's house at Gosford one day, when the Countess was conversing with him as to the acquirements of her daughters in art. The young ladies were meanwhile occupied in making grimaces at the odd man behind his back, forgetting that they were standing opposite a mirror, in which he could see all their movements. 'The young ladies', observed the painter, 'may have studied art, but I never saw such ugly faces as those they make', pointing to the glass before him.[50]

In addition, according to Thomas Carlyle, the artist gave the historian's future wife, Jane Baillie Welsh [137], drawing lessons as a young girl of fourteen, having previously drawn a portrait of her mother Grace and being a familiar figure in the Welsh household in Haddington:

> When it came to school-years, & she had to go to Edinburgh for her teaching, he openly expressed his encouragements, his determination to help her himself, with his best art, in the matter of Drawing, at least. She went accordingly to his grim Hermitage several times; found the cheerfullest welcome; the place very dusty, littery, idle-looking; and the man intent rather on talking to her, than on teaching with any diligence or clear method. Strange art-precepts he did give her here and there; which she could not then understand. The tasks he set her were impractical, his criticisms were rigorously severe. He liked far best to carry her about to the chosen Edinburgh friends he had, and shew her off, set her talking &c.[51]

The historian also recalled that Skirving was a practical man, being well-known for his unusual habit of making some of his own clothes. He also carved egg-cups from beef-bones, which he was in the habit of giving as presents, and made pieces of furniture. Carlyle treasured a gift from the artist to his wife of a fine mahogany drawing-board, which was incorporated into the main part of a table.

Skirving was clearly thought by his contemporaries to be an artist of outstanding talent, as well as notably proud, independent and eccentric. The respect in which he was held by many of his fellow younger artists is revealed by the number of times he was portrayed by them towards the end of his life. Notably he sat to Raeburn: the principal version of the portrait is in an American private collection [fig.27], while there also exists a smaller portrait painted from a slightly different angle [155, back cover]. George Watson portrayed Skirving twice in oils [153-4], and Andrew Geddes painted him in an oil portrait [157], as well as making an etched portrait to which Skirving appears to have added aquatint [158, fig.28]. Despite the parallels with Raeburn's career, and the mutual stylistic awareness between Skirving, Raeburn and Danloux during the second half of the 1790s, Skirving's influence on other artists was minimal. By contrast, Raeburn's increasing use of *chiaroscuro* lighting after 1800 made a considerable impact on Scottish portraiture for the rest of the nineteenth century. Only the young Sir David Wilkie in his early masterpiece, painted when he was nineteen, the forthright group portrait from 1804 of *William Chalmers Bethune, his Wife Isobel Morison and their Daughter Isabella* [fig.29], seems to have paid direct stylistic and aesthetic homage to Skirving rather than Raeburn, before he turned to his lucrative career in London as a painter of genre scenes.[52]

As most of Skirving's portraiture after his return from Italy was highly realistic in character and style, it is ironic that the artist's idealised posthumous drawing of *Robert Burns* [103], has become by far his best-known portrait. The unfinished copy in red chalk ('keel') of Nasmyth's oil portrayal of the poet [51, fig.30], whom Skirving never met, has always been considered a quintessential image of the poet. Skirving's pride in this portrait – and another of Burns's 'Highland Mary' – and his reluctance to sell them, notwith-

Fig.28: *Archibald Skirving c.*1815-19, by Andrew Geddes and Archibald Skirving [158]

Scottish National Portrait Gallery, Edinburgh

Fig.29: *William Chalmers Bethune, his Wife Isobel Morison and their Daughter Isabella* 1804, by Sir David Wilkie

National Gallery of Scotland, Edinburgh

Fig.30: *Robert Burns* 1787, by Alexander Nasmyth [51]

Scottish National Portrait Gallery, Edinburgh

standing many offers, are known from a letter he wrote to his brother in India on 17 June 1802. The letter also sheds light on the prices paid for his portraits, and his low productivity, which may have been due to recurring problems with his eyesight:

> I have been repeatedly offer'd 30 Guineas for a keel head of Burns, but it is not finished, and [is] still with me. It is taken from a picture (for I never saw him) in the hands of one I despise. I have been paid 30 [guineas] for heads in Crayons, and that only twice, a Lord Meadowbank and his son. But [I] am offered more than that for a Picture of Burns's Highland Mary, which I am sorry to part with. The chance is, it will be in London, long before your return. I am much pleased with it. – I work a little every day but it does not make 12 hours a week, so in this you are right. [53]

Skirving was correct in his prediction that there would be interest in his portrait of Burns from the connoisseurs and collectors in London. In June 1816 the artist made his last visit to London, staying for three to four months. During that trip he drew a few profile portraits in chalk, which are some of his last dated works [116-17, 159]. It is known that he met Scottish artists based in London, such as John Henning, the oil painter John Watson (later known as Sir John Watson Gordon), and the landscape painter Hugh William 'Grecian' Williams. He also met the sculptors Chantrey and Turnerelli, as well as the 'young Constable whom I found very obliging'. [54] Skirving also carried with him three letters of introduction from Sir Walter Scott, one of which gained him access to study the great collection of Old Master paintings belonging to the Marquess of Stafford. He also gained a meeting with Sir George Beaumont, the influential collector and arbiter of artistic taste, and an interview with the poet and critic Samuel Rogers. On 30 May 1816 Sir Walter Scott had written to Rogers from Edinburgh, introducing the eccentric artist to the sophisticated critic in a highly revealing account, which indicates that Skirving travelled with his portrait of Burns:

> Mr. Skirving of Edinburgh an unrivalled artist as a painter in crayons, is going to London with the only good portrait of Burns. I think you will like to look at it, and perhaps you may be even disposed to purchase it, provided the artist's intention of selling it holds good till he get to London. Mr. Skirving is a man of great genious [sic] in his art and is in circumstances of perfect independance [sic] although his dress unless he should rectify it when he gets [to] London would argue something very dificient. In fact both his dress and address requires all the allowance which genious [sic] knows how to make for the caprices and eccentricities of its brethren. Do not give yourself any trouble with him beyond what is exactly in the way of a lover of art. [55]

Scott concluded his letter to Rogers with a postscript that alludes to both the reputation of Skirving's 'keel' portrait of Burns and of the poet himself, also noting that his expenditure on altering his Borders estate at Abbotsford was preventing his own purchase of the drawing:

> I should think Mr. Sharpe would like to look at the Ayrshire ploughman. If Skirving does sell it, which appears to me very problematical, I wish this unique representation of our great poet to fall into good hands. If I had not been buying a sort of Oxmoor like Tristram Shandy and building hedging ditching & draining, Rob should not have crossed the Border. [56]

In the reply sent by Rogers to Scott on 13 July 1816, the critic sent his thanks for the 'introduction to Robert Burns, & to the Magician who has raised him again to life. To speak seriously, the Portrait is admirable, tho' I confess it would have affected my mind still more, if he had sat for it.' Rogers continued by mentioning Skirving: 'The Artist too struck me exceedingly. Such simplicity of manners I never saw; & he has great genius!' [57]

For the last three years of his life, Skirving mainly lived with his sister Grace [106] on her farm at Inveresk outside Musselburgh, and spent much of his time on long walks. He died suddenly on 19 May 1819, as was noted in a letter: 'Poor man, he was nailing some boards in an old pigeon house in his sister's garden when he fell down and instantly expired'. [58] He was buried in Athelstaneford churchyard in the same plot as his father and grandfather. Because of his extreme frugality during life, Skirving left a substantial personal estate of £4,006 10s.4d. This total figure included the very modest valuation of the artist's studio contents, made by William Bruce [168], rather than the considerably more substantial one made by the portraitist George Watson [169]. The artist's brother, Robert, who now farmed an estate at Croys in the Stewartry of Kirkcudbright, and his sister Grace, acted as the executors of his estate.[59]

Late in life, Thomas Carlyle, in his memoir of Archibald Skirving, empathised very strongly with two aspects of the artist's character, which were integral parts of his own personality. These have been described as 'rugged independence in all personal dealings and scorn for the world's opinion'. Carlyle also wrote of how, in 1821, as a young man he had visited the Skirving family tomb in the village of Athelstaneford. There, to this day, stands the tombstone bearing the epitaph, probably composed by the artist's brother Robert, which reads:

ARCHIBALD
BORN OCTOBER 1749
BY PECULIAR EXCELLENCE ATTAINED EMINENCE
AS A PORTRAIT PAINTER;
AND MIGHT HAVE LIVED IN AFFLUENCE,
HAD HE NOT AIMED AT PRIVATE INDEPENDENCE
BY SIMPLIFYING THE COMFORTS OF COMMON LIFE.

To beauty, virtue, talent, he would bow,
But claims from birth or rank would not allow;
Kept friends and foes at nearly equal distance:
Knew how to give, but not to take assistance.
At threescore-ten, when scarce begun to fail,
He dropt at once, without apparent ail.[60]

It was due to Archibald Skirving's proud and unyielding character that, unlike his great contemporary, the sociable and prolific Raeburn, he never won the artistic acclaim that was rightly his. It is only now, two hundred and fifty years after his birth, that Skirving is receiving the recognition that his exceptional skill and talent have for so long merited.

Notes and References

1 The 'Reminiscence of Adam and Archibald Skirving' was completed by Carlyle on 17 January 1868. The manuscript is now in the NLS (MS 1978, f.28) and was first published in 1974, cf. Carlyle 1974, p.136.

2 Goldie 1975, II, p.453; for Athelstaneford, cf. Duncan 1934 and King 1987.

3 Smiles 1862, II, p.278, n.1.

4 Cleghorn 1848, p.202.

5 Mackenzie 1927, p.212.

6 John Clubbe, the editor of the Carlyle manuscript, described seeing the miniature (oval, 2⅛in high), which was badly damaged, in the collection of Mrs Leila Hoskins at Cheltenham, cf. Carlyle 1974, p.132 and n.12.

7 For the Trustees Academy in Edinburgh, cf. Irwin & Irwin 1975, pp.90-7.

8 Three of these portraits are in the Art Gallery of New South Wales, Sydney, having been presented in 1956 by R.C. Scot Skirving, a collateral descendant of the artist. The *Self-portrait* (no.9247) measures 75.7 × 62.7cm; *Adam Skirving* (no.9245), 75.7 × 62.7cm; and *Christian Carnegie, Mrs Adam Skirving* (no.9246), 76.1 × 63.4cm, cf. Sydney 1981, Free 1987, pp.178-9, Scot Skirving 1988, pp.22-4, and Sundström 1994.

9 The qualities of precise drawing, subtle colouring and tightly observed character, can be seen in a number of other miniatures from this decade, now attributed to Raeburn. These include a pair of *James Gilliland* [26] and his wife *Elizabeth MacMurray, Mrs James Gilliland* [27], as well as a portrait of *George Sandilands of Strathtyrum* [28]. The significance of the pair of miniatures of Mr and Mrs James Gilliland was realised by William Zachs in 1997, and they were attributed to Raeburn by Duncan Thomson, being exhibited later

that year in the London showing of the 1997-8 *Raeburn* exhibition (ex-cat.), cf. Milner 1997 and Zachs 1998. I am grateful to David Mackie and Nicholas Phillipson for their comments. The Sandilands miniature was connected to Raeburn by Richard Walker. I am very grateful to him for drawing it to my attention. It was exhibited in the *Raeburn* exhibition in Edinburgh and London 1997-8 (ex-cat.). For Raeburn as a portrait miniaturist, cf. Irwin 1973.

10 Examples of Scottish miniatures from the late 1760s include *An Unknown Gentleman, thought to be Robert MacMurray* [19], together with a damaged, paired portrait of his wife; *William Cadell of Cockenzie* [18]; and *An Unknown Gentleman, possibly James Boswell* [20].

11 The letters of introduction – now destroyed – were seen by Basil Skinner in the possession of Mrs Leila Hoskins, cf. Skinner 1970, p.47. For Skirving's portraiture shown at the Royal Academy, listed under Archibald Shirving [*sic*], cf. Graves 1905-6, VII, pp.116-17, no.284. Skirving was only to exhibit once more at the Academy, in 1799 (no.836), the pastel 'Portrait of John Clerk of Elden [*sic*] Esq., author of the celebrated treatise on Naval Tactics' [92].

12 For a discussion of these artists and the growth of the market for portrait miniatures in the latter part of the 18th century, cf. Noon 1981, Foskett 1987 and Reynolds 1988. For Cosway, cf. Edinburgh and London 1995-6.

13 The details of the miniature in the Victoria & Albert Museum are: watercolour on ivory, oval, 7.3cm high, signed and dated on paper *Skirving [pinxi]t 1780*: Alan Evans bequest to the National Gallery, London, in 1974, transferred to the V&A Museum in 1995 (Evans 218).

14 Destroyed letter, formerly in the collection of Mrs Leila Hoskins, quoted in Skinner 1970, p.47.

15 Untraced letter quoted by Skinner 1970, p.48.

16 Cf. Edinburgh 1966, London 1974, London and Rome 1996-7 and Ingamells 1997.

17 Lord Elcho's letter of 6 January 1790, formerly in the Hoskins papers, cf. Skinner 1970, p.47.

18 Farington 1922-8, III, pp.53-4, 1790, for list of 21 artists; London, British Museum, Prints and Drawings Department, Whitley MSS, 1816, letter sent from Rome, dated 20 April 1794; London, British Library, MS.Add.36497, ff.290-91, for Skirving's letter to Cumberland, 5 March 1794; London, British Library, Mrs Flaxman's Journal, MS.Add.39792, regular entries to Sherwin [*sic*] from February 1791 to March 1792.

19 Edinburgh, National Library of Scotland, Forbes Journal MS, 29 November 1792, 23 November 1792, 23 March 1793 (Lusieri) and April 1793 (Tischbein), quoted in Skinner 1970, p.49. Skinner also noted that he had seen Skirving's manuscript notebook, compiled in Rome during 1789 (formerly in the Hoskins papers).

20 Gardenstone 1802, III, pp.152-3.

21 For Archibald Skirving's letter of 18 December 1790, formerly in the Hoskins papers, cf. Skinner 1970, p.47.

22 Cleghorn 1848, II, p.203.

23 Edinburgh University Library, Laing Papers, MS.La.IV.25.

24 Raeburn's use of a deep shadow on the brow can be seen in works such as *David Hunter of Blackness* of c.1788, *William Tytler of Woodhouselee* from c.1789, *Sir John and Lady Clerk of*

Penicuik of 1791-2 and *The Revd Robert Walker ('The Skating Minister')* from the mid-1790s, cf. Irwin & Irwin 1975, pp.146-64; Mackie 1994; Thomson 1994; and Duncan Thomson, 'Sir Henry Raeburn: An Introduction to his Life and Art' in Edinburgh and London 1997-8, pp.11-22, and cat.nos.2-4, 8, 13 and 19.

25 Edinburgh 1995, p.8, fig.1 (col.); a studio connection between Archibald Skirving and Hugh Douglas Hamilton has even been proposed, cf. Skinner 1970, p.49.

26 I am grateful to Margaret Mackay for identifying the Fontana dei Cavalli Marini in the Borghese Gardens.

27 Observed by Lindsay Stainton in her catalogue entry on this drawing, London 1974, no.18. Ingres's portrait drawings of tourists to Rome, mainly British, were made principally during his long first stay there from 1806 to 1824, especially after the final defeat of Napoleon in 1815, and the ensuing return of visitors to Italy (cf. Naef 1956 and Naef 1977-80).

28 Cleghorn 1848, II, p.203.

29 Letter of 17 June 1802, quoted in Skinner 1970, p.50. Skirving may have suffered from the eye condition known as uniocular diplopia.

30 'Il nous paroît aussi de la justice et de la droiture de faire connaître en France que le nomé Shirvin [*sic*], natif d'Ecosse, qui a été puis sur le même navire, a souffert et souffrer encore de la tiranie anglaise une atrosse persécution pour la cause de la liberté. C'est artiste nous a toujours manifesté à Rome l'amour la plus grande pour la Révolution française'; 'Je t'ai rendu compte dans le temps de l'emprisonnement au château Saint-Ange du citoyen de War, sculpteur flamand ... il a été pris par mer ... le peintre écossais pris avec lui paroît aussi mériter des égards, suivant le témoignage que de nos patriotes rendent de son caractère et de son amour pour notre révolution...', cf. Montaiglon & Guiffrey 1887-1912, XVI, pp.383 and 385; and also cf. Ingamells 1997, pp.863 and 867.

31 Smiles 1862, II, p.278, n.1.

32 Carlyle 1974, p.132.

33 NLS, MS 10102.m-p. In 1802 Skirving sold the appartment for £600 to the lawyer Adam Wilson. A year later Skirving also inherited a property in Haddington from his father.

34 Statements quoted in Skinner 1970, p.50.

35 Carlyle 1974, pp.133-4.

36 Gibson 1816, p.480.

37 Mackenzie 1927, p.213.

38 Cleghorn 1848, II, p.204.

39 Lord Woodhouselee was also shown among his family in a watercolour of 1804 by his eldest daughter Anne Fraser Tytler [111].

40 Cleghorn 1848, II, 204.

41 Cunningham quoted by Cleghorn 1848, II, p.205.

42 Mackenzie 1927, p.212.

43 The poet James Hogg, 'the Ettrick Shepherd', referred to Skirving as 'whimsical' in his 1821 collection of Scottish songs, *The Jacobite Relics of Scotland* [58]; Gibson 1816, p.480.

44 NLS, Minto Papers, MS 11909, ff.120-21.

45 Portalis 1910; Smailes 1985.

46 Edinburgh and London 1997-8, pp.88-91, no.19 and pp.114-15, no.30.

47 For the miniature of Danloux, cf. Portalis 1910, p.459, ill.

48 Foskett 1974, pp.15 and 27; Brown 1995, p.11.

49 Cleghorn 1848, II, p.204.

50 Smiles 1862, II, p.278, n.1.

51 Carlyle 1974, p.135.

52 Errington 1988, p.7, pl.1.

53 A photocopy of the 1802 letter is preserved in the accession file (SNPG archive) on the 'keel' head of *Robert Burns* [103]. This is the only known photocopy made from 'mass of old letters' by and relating to Skirving, formerly in the Hoskins papers. The letter is partially quoted in Skinner 1970, p.51.

54 Quoted in Skinner 1970, p.51.

55 Scott 1932-7, IV, pp.243-4.

56 Ibid.

57 Ibid.

58 Quoted in Skinner 1970, p.52.

59 NLS, MS 10102.i-k, 'State of Archd Skirvings personal Estates', 'State of the Personal Estate of the late Archibald Skirving Esquire' and 'State of A Skirving Esqre Debts and General expenses 1819'. An 'Inventory of the personal Estate of Archibald Skirving', late 'portrait painter in Edinburgh' can be found in Edinburgh, Scottish Record Office, SC70/1/19, ff.540-44 and CC8/8/145, ff.157v-158v.

60 Carlyle 1974, pp.132-7 and Clubbe in op. cit., p.127. The artist's epitaph is preceded by those of his father and grandfather, Adam and Archibald: ARCHIBALD SKIRVING / FARMER. MUIRTON. / ONE OF THE MOST ATHLETIC AND BEST TEMPERED / OF MEN / *His Oldest Son*, ADAM. / *Farmer. Garleton. / Born 1719. / Died 1803. / In feature, in figure, agility, mind, / And happy wit, rarely surpass'd / With lofty or low could be plain or refined, / Content becoming bright to the last.*

PLATE I
Archibald Skirving *Adam Skirving c.*1770
[42]

PLATE 2
Unknown Scottish Artist
An Unknown Gentleman, possibly James Boswell c.1765–70
[20]

PLATE 3
Attributed to Sir Henry Raeburn
James Gilliland c.1775
[26]

PLATE 4
Attributed to Archibald Skirving
Anne Biddulph, Mrs Gordon c.1785
[35]

PLATE 5
Attributed to Archibald Skirving
*The Hon. Clementina Sarah Drummond
(later Baroness Willoughby de Eresby) c.1798*
[125]

PLATE 6
Archibald Skirving *Gavin Hamilton* 1788–9
[60]

PLATE 7
Archibald Skirving *Francis Charteris, Viscount Elcho of Amisfield* 1790
[62]

PLATE 8
Archibald Skirving *William Craig, Lord Craig* c.1796–1801
[89]

PLATE 9
Archibald Skirving *Janet Skirving, Mrs James Carnegie of Edrom Newton* c.1796–1803
[85]

PLATE 10
Archibald Skirving *Robert Boswell of St Boswells c.*1795-6
[84]

PLATE II
Archibald Skirving after Henri-Pierre Danloux *Mary Drummond, Mrs John Pringle of Stitchell* *c.*1798
[86]

PLATE 12
Archibald Skirving *Henry Home Drummond, 6th Laird of Blair Drummond c.1798*

PLATE 13
Archibald Skirving *Mrs Johnston of Hutton Hall c.*1796–1800
[88]

PLATE 14
Archibald Skirving *Margaret Sym, Mrs John Wilson* c.1797–1800
[90]

PLATE 16
Archibald Skirving *John Clerk of Eldin* 1799–1800

[92]

PLATE 19
Archibald Skirving after Alexander Nasmyth *Robert Burns* 1796–8
[103]

CATALOGUE

The Catalogue is divided into four sections:

1 · East Lothian, Edinburgh and London 1749–1786

2 · Italy and France 1787–1795

3 · Edinburgh, London and East Lothian 1795–1819

4 · Image and Reputation

In each section the works are grouped chronologically in the following order: pastels (or crayons); drawings; miniatures; oils; prints; other items. The terms pastel and crayon are interchangeable and are used below accordingly. While the terms pastels and pastellist are more common today, the 18th- and early 19th-century terminology of 'crayon-painter' or 'painter in crayons' is still sometimes used. All works are on paper unless described otherwise.

Abbreviations

NGS

National Gallery of Scotland, Edinburgh

NLS

National Library of Scotland, Edinburgh

RSA

Royal Scottish Academy, Edinburgh

SNPG

Scottish National Portrait Gallery, Edinburgh

Maurice-Quentin de La Tour 1702–84

1 ***Prince Charles Edward Stewart 1748***

Pastel, 61 × 51cm (24 × 20⅛in)
Provenance: Townley Hall, Ireland; Christie's, London, 10 June 1994, lot 25; purchased with the assistance of the National Art Collections Fund
Exhibited: Paris 1748, no.80 ('Le Prince Edouard')
Literature: Nicholas 1973, pp.34-5
SCOTTISH NATIONAL PORTRAIT GALLERY

Maurice-Quentin de La Tour was one of the finest of the 18th-century pastellists, and his portraits were noted for their combination of searching characterisation and light textures. His work had an influence on Allan Ramsay's portraiture of the 1750s [2]. De La Tour's portrait of the Young Pretender, drawn in exile in Paris after the disastrous battle of Culloden, was exhibited at the Salon in 1748. The frame is original. In later life Prince Charles Edward Stewart (1720-88) was painted in oils by Hugh Douglas Hamilton [49].

Allan Ramsay 1713–84

2 ***Self-portrait c.1755–6***

Pastel and watercolour, 40.6 × 28.2cm (16 × 11⅛in)
Provenance: presented by the RSA in 1910
Exhibited: Edinburgh and London 1992-3, p.120, no.52 and col. frontispiece
Literature: Smailes 1990, pp.240-1, ill.
SCOTTISH NATIONAL PORTRAIT GALLERY

This pastel self-portrait by Allan Ramsay was probably drawn in Rome, and is a rare example of Ramsay's use of this medium. It shows the influence of the French crayon-painter Maurice-Quentin de La Tour [1]. Ramsay made four extended visits to Rome between 1736 and 1784.

Francis Cotes 1726–90

3 ***Sir William Chambers 1764***

Pastel, 63.5 × 48.2cm (25 × 19in)
Signed and dated on recto: *FCotes pxt. / 1764*
Provenance: General Sir Redvers Buller; purchased in 1904
Literature: Russell 1777, p.18; Smailes 1990, pp.63-4, ill.
SCOTTISH NATIONAL PORTRAIT GALLERY

Sir William Chambers (1726-96), who was of Scottish descent, became one of the foremost neo-classical architects in Britain. Francis Cotes worked as a pastellist in London during the 1750s and early 1760s. He was influenced by Jean-Étienne Liotard, during his first visit to London (1753-5). Cotes also taught the pastellist John Russell (1745-1806), who, together with Daniel Gardner (1750-1805), dominated the market for 'crayon-paintings' in London during the last three decades of the 18th century. This pastel is in the original 'Maratta' type frame.

Attributed to Archibald Skirving after David Martin 1737–98

4 ***Henry Dundas (later 1st Viscount Melville) c.1770–80***

[fig.6]
Pastel, feigned oval, 44.4 × 38.7cm (17½ × 15¼in)
Provenance: by family descent
THE DUNDAS-BEKKER FAMILY, ARNISTON HOUSE

This is a partial copy (head and shoulders) after David Martin's three-quarter length portrait of *Henry Dundas* (1742-1811), painted in 1770, which is now in the Scottish National Portrait Gallery (PG 2745). Dundas was born into one of Scotland's most powerful legal and political families. Trained as a lawyer, he went on to become virtual ruler of Scotland for thirty years, until his impeachment trial in 1806. He had acted as Pitt's right-hand man north of the Border. One of his younger cousins was Robert Dundas of Arniston (1797-1838), who was portrayed by Skirving as a child in a full-length pastel [95].

Attributed to Archibald Skirving

5 ***An Unknown Girl c.1770–80***

[fig.7]
Pastel, 53.3 × 43.2cm (21 × 17in)
Provenance: by family descent; Mrs A.A. Scot Skirving
Exhibited: Edinburgh 1955, no.87
Literature: Sundström 1994
ELISABETH A. McINTYRE

This charming portrait of a young girl, drawn in a feigned oval, has descended from collateral relations of the artist. It can be dated to the 1770s on account of the costume and head-dress (information from Rosalind Marshall). The rather flat effects of the pastel can be compared to similar characteristics, in his miniatures painted in London [31, 35, fig.9].

Catherine Read 1723–78

6 ***Three Children of Henry, 3rd Duke of Buccleuch 1773***

Pastel, oval, 76 × 54.2cm (29⅞ × 21⅜in)
Inscribed on label on verso: *Miss Catherine Read &c / Children of Henry Duke of Buccleuch*
Provenance: by family descent
Exhibited: Royal Academy, London 1773, no.229 ('Three Children; in crayons'); London 1939, no.50
Literature: Manners 1932, pp.37-40, fig.III
THE RT HON. THE EARL OF HOME CVO, CBE

The three children of Henry, 3rd Duke of Buccleuch (1746-1812), are, from left to right: Lady Elizabeth Scott, who married Alexander Home, 10th Earl of Home [65]; Lady Mary Scott, who married the 3rd Earl of Courtown; and Charles, the Earl of Dalkeith, who succeeded his father as 4th Duke of Buccleuch. The sitters can also be seen as adults in Danloux's 1798 conversation piece in oils of *Henry, 3rd Duke of Buccleuch and his Family* [139]. Catherine Read was a Scottish artist who, after studying in Paris and Rome, after 1754 made a successful career as a pastellist in London. She went to India in 1775, where she died. Read is the only significant Scottish pastellist to compare with Skirving during the 18th century, though their widely contrasting styles epitomise the difference between the rococo and neo-classical aesthetic.

Ozias Humphry 1742–1810

7 *Gavin Hamilton* **1777**

Pencil, 53.1 × 43.1cm (20⅞ × 17in)
Signed in monogram and dated on recto: OH /
1777
Provenance: presented by the Earl of Stair in
1887
Literature: Lloyd Williams 1994, ill. frontis-
piece
SCOTTISH NATIONAL PORTRAIT GALLERY

Previously thought to be a self-portrait of
Gavin Hamilton (1723–98), due to the
discovery by Timothy Clifford of a signa-
ture and a date, this drawing can now be
identified as a work of Ozias Humphry
from 1777. Mainly known as a fashionable
miniaturist in London [23], Humphry
spent much of the 1770s in Italy, before
continuing his career in India. After
returning to London, he worked mainly
as a pastellist. This drawing can be contrasted with the later pastel of Hamilton
by Skirving [60]. Gavin Hamilton spent
most of the last forty years of his life in
Rome.

John Brown 1749–87

8 *George Paton* **c.1780–1**

Pencil, oval, 10.5cm (4⅛in) high
Provenance: purchased in 1887
Literature: Smailes 1990, pp.231 and 233, ill.
SCOTTISH NATIONAL PORTRAIT GALLERY

This drawing by John Brown of the anti-
quary George Paton (1721–1807) was one
of the first made by the artist after his
return from Italy in 1780, where he had
stayed for nine years.

Archibald Skirving

9 *A Seated Gentleman with his Arm
over the Back of a Chair* **c.1780–6**

Red chalk, 39.3 × 25.2cm (15⅜ × 10in)
Inscribed on recto in pencil with initials: AS
Provenance: presented by Miss Bruce of
Edinburgh in 1938
Literature: Andrews & Brotchie 1960, p.219
NATIONAL GALLERY OF SCOTLAND

This informal and slightly mechanical
study by Skirving of a man leaning over
the back of a chair may date from before
the artist's visit to Italy at the end of 1786.
The verso shows a study of a seated man
in an officer's uniform.

Archibald Skirving

10 *A Seated Lady* **c.1780–6**

Pencil and black chalk, 21.1 × 19.4cm
(8¼ × 7¾in)
Provenance: presented by Miss Bruce of
Edinburgh in 1938
Literature: Andrews & Brotchie 1960, p.220
NATIONAL GALLERY OF SCOTLAND

As with the drawing of an unknown gentleman looking over the back of a chair
[9], this informal study of an unknown
lady seated by a stove is likely to date from
before Skirving's visit to Italy in 1786.

John Brown 1749–87

11 *David Steuart Erskine, 11th Earl of
Buchan* **c.1781**

Pencil, 49.8 × 35.1cm (19⅝ × 13⅞in)
Inscribed on recto: *Earl of Buchan*
Provenance: one of a series of portrait drawings
commissioned by the Society of Antiquaries of
Scotland in 1781; on loan since 1882
Literature: Smailes 1990, pp.45 and 47, ill.
SOCIETY OF ANTIQUARIES OF SCOTLAND,
EDINBURGH [ON LOAN TO THE SCOTTISH
NATIONAL PORTRAIT GALLERY]

Lord Buchan, a leading antiquarian,
praised Skirving and his works in a letter
to the Hon. Gilbert Elliot of c.1809 (NLS,
Minto Papers, MS 11909, ff.120–21).

John Brown 1749–87

12 *The Revd Alexander Carlyle* **c.1781**

Pencil, 60.6 × 41.6cm (23⅞ × 16⅜in)
Provenance: purchased in 1961
Literature: Smailes 1990, pp.57 and 59, ill.
SCOTTISH NATIONAL PORTRAIT GALLERY

This drawing of the noted divine and
pamphleteer, the Revd Alexander Carlyle
(1722–1805), by John Brown, can be compared to Skirving's portrait in oils of the
same sitter [143]. Skirving – an exact
contemporary of Brown – also drew
Carlyle in a profile portrait drawing of
c.1800, which is on long-term loan from
the Kirk Session of Inveresk to the Scottish National Portrait Gallery (PGL 154).
Brown's portrait drawings can be compared to Skirving's essays made in this
format from 1793 [fig.15] until 1816 [116–
17].

John Brown 1749–87

13 *Alexander Runciman* **1785**

Pencil, 7.3 × 9.5cm (2⅞ × 3¾in)
Signed and dated on recto: *Runciman Pictor –* /
J. Brown Delt. ad vivam [sic] / *1785*; inscribed
on book: *Ossian*
Provenance: Society of Antiquaries of Scotland;
on loan since 1882
Literature: Smailes 1990, pp.249–50, ill.
SOCIETY OF ANTIQUARIES OF SCOTLAND,
EDINBURGH [ON LOAN TO THE SCOTTISH
NATIONAL PORTRAIT GALLERY]

Both John Brown and Alexander
Runciman (1736–85) – like Skirving –
made extended visits to Italy, in
Runciman's case from 1767 to 1771. The
inscription on the book refers to
Runciman undertaking an ambitious
series of narrative paintings on Ossian
for Sir James Clerk at Penicuik House
(destroyed by fire in 1899).

John Brown 1749–87

14 *Jane Maxwell, Duchess of Gordon*
1786

Pencil, 13 × 8.2cm (5⅛ × 3¼in)
Provenance: purchased in 1931
Literature: Smailes 1990, pp.123 and 125, ill.
SCOTTISH NATIONAL PORTRAIT GALLERY

This portrait of Jane Maxwell (c.1749–
1812), wife of the 4th Duke of Gordon, is
an example of John Brown's fine pencil
portraiture after his return from Italy in
1780 [11, 13, 15].

John Brown 1749–87

15 *David Deuchar* **1787**

Pencil, 5.3 × 4.6cm (2⅛ × 1⅞in)
Inscribed and dated on verso: *[Sea]l Engraver
[-] / by Mr. John Brow[n] / 1787*
Provenance: bequeathed by Miss Jane Deuchar
in 1925
Literature: Smailes 1990, pp.86 and 89, ill.
SCOTTISH NATIONAL PORTRAIT GALLERY

This classicizing profile portrait of the
seal engraver David Deuchar (1743–1808)
can be compared to Raeburn's earlier
portrait miniature of the sitter from 1773
[24].

Robert Barker 1739–1806

16 *Panoramic View of Edinburgh from
Calton Hill* **1792**

Watercolour, 41 × 326cm (16¼ × 128⅜in)
Signed and dated on recto in pen and ink:
R. Barker delt. / 1792
Exhibited: Edinburgh 1995, p.110
UNIVERSITY OF EDINBURGH LIBRARY

This panoramic view of Edinburgh from Calton Hill is a reduced version of one of the earliest exhibited panoramas (1789), which was engraved later that year by J. Wells in six separate aquatints (City Art Centre, Edinburgh; cf. Bonn 1993, p.732, no.II.25). The Old Town can be contrasted with the recently built New Town, while in the centre of the composition the viewer looks down onto Leith Street (or Terrace) and behind it St James's Square, where Skirving had his studio and apartment after his return from Italy. Berwick Law, a prominent geological feature of the artist's native East Lothian, can be glimpsed to the far right of the panorama.

Gervase Spencer d.1763 after Allan Ramsay 1713–84

17 *Lady Katherine Gordon c.*1750

Enamel set onto lid of gold and enamelled snuff-box by Jean-Joseph Barrière, 1775–81, with original shagreen box, oval, 5.5cm (2⅛in) high
Provenance: by family descent
THE RT HON. THE EARL OF WEMYSS & MARCH, KT

Lady Katherine Gordon (d.1786) married the Hon. Francis Charteris of Amisfield (1725–1808), who, in 1787, became 7th Earl of Wemyss [23, 30, fig.4]. This enamel was copied from the full-length portrait of the couple, painted by Allan Ramsay in *c.*1750 (Wemyss collection, Gosford House).

Unknown Scottish Artist

18 *William Cadell of Cockenzie c.*1760–70

Watercolour on ivory, oval, 2.5cm (1in) high
Engraved on verso: *Willm. Cadell / of Cockenzie / Died March 1777 / Aged 78. / Christian Cadell / relect of Thos. Edington / Died 10. Decr. 1814. / aged 72.*
Provenance: by family descent
MAJOR MALCOLM R.S. MACRAE, SKAILL HOUSE, ORKNEY

This portrait of William Cadell (1699–1777) by an unknown Scottish miniaturist, with its careful drawing and colouring, may be compared to similarly painted miniatures from the 1760s: *An Unknown Gentleman, thought to be Robert MacMurray* [19] and *An Unknown Gentleman, possibly James Boswell* [20]. Portraits such as these provide a context for understanding the origins of Skirving and Raeburn's emergence as miniaturists in Edinburgh during the early 1770s.

Unknown Scottish Artist

19 *An Unknown Gentleman, thought to be Robert MacMurray c.*1760–70

Watercolour on ivory, oval, 5.1cm (2in) high
Provenance: by family descent
Exhibited: London 1998
Literature: Zachs 1998, pl.2a
JOHN MURRAY

This portrait, which can be dated to the 1760s on the grounds of the sitter's dress and the artist's tightly-drawn style, can be linked to miniatures of a similar date, such as *An Unknown Gentleman, possibly James Boswell* [20] and *William Cadell of Cockenzie* [18]. Works such as these foreshadow the early miniatures of Skirving and Raeburn. The probable sitter, Robert MacMurray, was the father of John Murray I, the eminent Edinburgh-born publisher, who later enjoyed a successful career in London.

Unknown Scottish Artist

20 *An Unknown Gentleman, possibly James Boswell c.*1765–70

[colour plate 2]
Watercolour on ivory, 5.1cm (2in) high
Provenance: by family descent
PRIVATE COLLECTION

This miniature, with its frank characterisation and carefully drawn technique, is close in style to miniatures painted in Edinburgh during the early careers of Skirving and Raeburn. While it may be compared with Skirving's portrait miniature of his father *Adam Skirving* [fig.1] and Raeburn's early works, such as the *David Deuchar* [24], *James Gilliland* [26], *Elizabeth MacMurray, Mrs James Gilliland* [27] and *George Sandilands of Strathtyrum* [28], its dating from costume and wig to the late 1760s would preclude an attribution to either of these

artists (information from Rosalind Marshall). The sitter, with his fleshy appearance and melancholic expression, bears a resemblance to other portraits of the biographer James Boswell (1740–95), in particular George Willison's oil executed in Rome during 1765, now in the Scottish National Portrait Gallery, Edinburgh (PG 804; Edinburgh and London 1967, no.18). The miniature, which belongs to Boswell's collateral descendants, is framed with other miniatures of a woman, three boys and one girl, dating from the 1770s.

John Bogle c.1746–1803

21 *Commodore George Johnstone c.*1767–74

Watercolour on ivory, 9.9cm (3⅞in) high
Signed on recto: *I Bogle / Pinxt*
Provenance: Edward Grosvenor Paine; purchased in 1982
Exhibited: Edinburgh and London 1995–6, p.115, no.23, col. pl.
Literature: Smailes 1990, pp.161–2, ill.
SCOTTISH NATIONAL PORTRAIT GALLERY

This miniature of Commodore Johnstone (1730–87), the naval commander and governor of Western Florida, is John Bogle's masterpiece. The intense realism of the portrait can be compared to Skirving's mature work in pastel from the 1790s and early 1800s.

James Scouler c.1740–1812

22 *An Unknown Lady* 1768

Watercolour on ivory, oval, 7.6cm (3in) high
Signed and dated on recto: *J. Scouler*; inscribed in pen and ink on verso: *this paper not to be taken off / 1768*
PRIVATE COLLECTION

James Scouler (or Scoular), born in Edinburgh, made a successful career as a miniaturist in London. His portraits are painted in a realistic style, similar to the work of John Bogle [21, 32–4], George Engleheart [29] and John Smart. These were in contrast to the lighter-toned miniatures being produced by Skirving during his London period, when he was influenced by the fashionable work of Richard Cosway [30, 38, fig.4].

Ozias Humphry 1742–1810

23 *The Hon. Francis Charteris of Amisfield (later 7th Earl of Wemyss)* 1771

Watercolour on ivory in gold clasp with diamond setting, oval, 3cm (1¼in) high
Signed on recto in monogram: OH; engraved on gold verso: *F.C. Senr. / Ozias Humphry / 1771*
Provenance: by family descent
Literature: Gosford House, Muniment Room, Account Books, 14 August 1771 ('Paid Ozias Humphry in London for portrait in miniature 12 gns.')
THE RT HON. THE EARL OF WEMYSS & MARCH, KT

The Hon. Francis Charteris of Amisfield (1725–1808) was the landlord of the farm at East Garleton, near Haddington, where Skirving was born and brought up. Ozias Humphry was one of the leading miniaturists active in London during the 1760s and 1770s, before he went to find work in India. It is likely that Skirving would have been well aware of Humphry's portrait miniatures during his stay in London from 1778. The sitter was also portrayed in miniature by Richard Cosway in 1779 [30, fig.4]. As a younger man he was painted by Allan Ramsay in *c.*1750 in a full-length double-portrait with his wife Lady Katherine Gordon.

Sir Henry Raeburn 1756–1823

24 *David Deuchar c.*1773

Watercolour on ivory, oval, 6cm (2⅜in) high
Inscribed on verso: *David Deuchar, Esq., / of Morningside, / by Sir Henry Raeburn, / being the second portrait done by him, / during the time he was / an apprentice with Mr. Gilland [Gilliland], / Jeweller, Parliament Square / Edinburgh / Painted about 1773*
Provenance: by descent in the sitter's family; the Revd J. Seton Deuchar; purchased in 1931
Exhibited: Edinburgh and London 1997–8, p.47, no.1, col. pl.
Literature: Irwin 1973, p.243; NGS 1996, p.286, ill.
NATIONAL GALLERY OF SCOTLAND

This miniature of the goldsmith, seal engraver and amateur etcher David Deuchar (1743–1808) is a touchstone for attributing Raeburn's early miniatures. The sitter was later portrayed in 1787 in a miniature profile drawing by John Brown [15]. Raeburn studied in Rome from 1784 to 1786.

Samuel Cotes 1734–1818

25 *John Hay c.*1771–2

Watercolour on ivory in gold bracelet clasp frame, oval, 3.8cm (1½in) high
Engraved on gold verso: JOHN HAY / Aged 63
Provenance: purchased with the assistance of the National Art Collections Fund in 1996
Literature: NACF *Review* 1996, p.172, col. pl.; *Burlington Magazine* 1997, p.582, ill.
SCOTTISH NATIONAL PORTRAIT GALLERY

This is a characteristic work from the 1770s by the Irish miniaturist, who, like his better-known brother, Francis Cotes, the pastellist and oil painter, established himself in London. In 1746 John Hay (d.1781) was appointed secretary to Prince Charles Edward Stewart [1, 49]. Later, in exile, he was made master of the Prince's household and a baronet of Scotland. He received a royal pardon from George III in 1771.

Attributed to Sir Henry Raeburn 1756–1823

26 *James Gilliland c.*1775

[colour plate 3]
Watercolour on ivory (cracked), 5.1cm (2in) high
Provenance: by family descent
Exhibited: Edinburgh and London 1997–8 (London only), ex-cat.
Literature: Milner 1997; Zachs 1998, pl.2b (left)
JOHN MURRAY

This miniature, whose significance was realised by William Zachs, and which was attributed to Raeburn by Duncan Thomson, is almost certainly a rare surviving early work by Raeburn, especially when compared to the artist's generally accepted portrait of *David Deuchar* [24] of *c.*1773. James Gilliland was an Edinburgh jeweller and goldsmith, to whom Raeburn was apprenticed. There is a pair to this miniature of the sitter's wife, *Elizabeth MacMurray, Mrs James Gilliland* [27]. This miniature has recently been conserved.

Attributed to Sir Henry Raeburn 1756–1823

27 *Elizabeth MacMurray, Mrs James Gilliland c.*1775

Watercolour on ivory, oval, 5.1cm (2in) high
Provenance: by family descent
Literature: Zachs 1998, ill.
Exhibited: Edinburgh and London 1997–8 (London only), ex-cat.
JOHN MURRAY

The sitter was the daughter of Robert MacMurray [19] and the sister of the publisher John Murray I, the founder of the famous London publishing house (Zachs 1998).

Attributed to Sir Henry Raeburn 1756–1823

28 *George Sandilands of Strathtyrum c.*1775

Watercolour on ivory (cracked), oval, 3.9cm (1½in) high
Provenance: by family descent
Exhibited: Edinburgh and London 1997–8, ex-cat.
PRIVATE COLLECTION

This miniature of George Sandilands of Strathtyrum (1755–1824), which was first attributed to Raeburn by Richard Walker, can be confidently linked to the same artist's portrait from *c.*1773 of the seal engraver *David Deuchar* [24]. Notable shared characteristics are the careful drawing and delicate shading.

George Engleheart 1750/3–1829

29 *Mrs Bazett c.*1775

Watercolour on ivory, oval, 3.9cm (1½in) high
Signed on recto lower left with initials: GE
Provenance: by family descent
PRIVATE COLLECTION

Little is known of the sitter, except that she was a close friend of Lady Muncaster, wife of John, 1st Baron Muncaster (1737–1813). This portrait is a particularly sharp image produced by one of the most successful and prolific miniaturists working in London from the 1770s onwards, at a time when Skirving was attempting to establish himself as a miniaturist in the metropolis.

Richard Cosway 1742–1821

30 *The Hon. Francis Charteris of Amisfield (later 7th Earl of Wemyss)* 1779

[fig.4]
Watercolour on ivory, re-set in 1787 with diamonds and enamel, hair setting and earl's coronet on verso, with original red leather case, oval, 4.3 cm (1⅝ in)
Diamond monogram on verso: cw [Charteris-Wemyss]
Provenance: by family descent
Literature: Gosford House, Muniment Room, Account Books, entry for 1779 ('Rich. Cosway picture of myself and setting it in gold £17/17/-')
THE RT HON. THE EARL OF WEMYSS & MARCH, KT

The Hon. Francis Charteris of Amisfield (1725–1808), the Skirving family's landlord, became the 7th Earl of Wemyss in 1787, when this spectacular diamond and enamelled setting was added to Cosway's miniature of 1779. The sitter had already been portrayed in a miniature eight years earlier by Ozias Humphry [23], who, like Cosway, was a leading miniaturist in London during the 1770s. Skirving would have been very conscious of these two miniaturists during his stay in London from 1778. Francis Charteris, as a younger man, and his wife Lady Katherine Gordon [17] had been portrayed in a full-length oil by Allan Ramsay in c.1750 (Wemyss collection, Gosford House).

Attributed to Archibald Skirving

31 *An Unknown Lady* c.1780–85

Watercolour on ivory, oval, 7.6cm (3in) high
Monogram in gold on verso: CR
Provenance: Christie's, London, 23 May 1989, lot III
PRIVATE COLLECTION

This miniature by Skirving of an unknown lady holding a mask is particularly close in style, composition and date to the miniature of *An Unknown Lady* [fig.9] – signed and dated 1780 – in the Victoria & Albert Museum, and to a lesser extent to that of *Anne Biddulph, Mrs Gordon* [35], which can be dated to around 1785.

John Bogle c.1746–1803

32 *An Unknown Gentleman* 1781

Watercolour on ivory, oval, 3.5cm (1⅜in) high
Signed and dated on recto: I.B. / 1781
Provenance: NGS; transferred in 1982
Literature: Smailes 1990, p.352
SCOTTISH NATIONAL PORTRAIT GALLERY

John Bogle c.1746–1803

33 *An Unknown Gentleman* 1782

Watercolour on ivory, oval, 3.8cm (1½in) high
Signed and dated on recto: I.B. / 1782
PRIVATE COLLECTION

The Scottish miniaturist John Bogle made a successful career in London from c.1770 to 1800, producing portraits [21, 32, 34] in a highly realistic style, similar to those of George Englehart [29] and John Smart. This was in contrast to Skirving's attempts during his period in London to paint lighter miniatures, under the influence of Richard Cosway [30, 38, fig.4].

John Bogle c.1746–1803

34 *An Unknown Gentleman* 1784

Watercolour on ivory, oval, 3.5cm (1⅜in) high
Signed and dated on recto: I.B. / 1784
Provenance: NGS; transferred in 1982
Literature: Smailes 1990, p.352
SCOTTISH NATIONAL PORTRAIT GALLERY

Attributed to Archibald Skirving

35 *Anne Biddulph, Mrs Gordon* c.1785

[colour plate 4]
Watercolour on ivory, oval, 7.9cm (3⅛in) high
Provenance: Robert Bayne-Powell; Christie's, London, 21 April 1998, lot III
PRIVATE COLLECTION

Although not signed, this large miniature can be confidently attributed to Skirving on account of its compositional and stylistic similarity to two signed miniatures of unknown ladies, one in the Victoria & Albert Museum [fig.9], the other in a private collection [31]. The delicate brushwork, the spectacularly fashionable plumed hat and the blue sky background all indicate that Skirving was well aware of the work of Richard Cosway (1742–1821), the leading miniaturist in London during the 1780s. A similar miniature by Skirving from this date of an unknown lady in a plumed hat is in a private collection (Foskett 1987, p.340, col. pl.27A).

Charles Shirreff b. c.1750

36 *An Unknown Officer* 1785

Watercolour on ivory, oval, 6.4cm (2½in) high
PRIVATE COLLECTION

Charles Shirreff was a Scottish miniaturist who made his career in London before working in India, like a number of other miniaturists at this period including Ozias Humphry and John Smart.

Sir Henry Raeburn 1756–1823 after Hugh Douglas Hamilton c.1739–1808

37 *George John Spencer, 2nd Earl Spencer* 1785

Oil on ivory, oval, 6.7 × 5.5cm (2⅝ × 2⅛in)
Provenance: by family descent
Exhibited: Edinburgh and London 1997–8, p.54, no.4, col. pl.
Literature: Foskett 1972, I, p.460, II, pl.283; Irwin 1973, p.243, fig.64
ALTHORP PARK

This is a unique surviving example of a portrait miniature painted by Raeburn during his Italian visit (1784–6). Despite being a copy – from an untraced pastel by the Irish artist Hugh Douglas Hamilton, whose style is close to Skirving's – and being painted in a highly unusual medium, it provides useful comparative evidence for miniatures painted by Skirving in Rome (1787–94).

Richard Cosway 1742–1821

38 *Charles Anderson-Pelham, 1st Baron Yarborough* [recto]; *Charles Anderson-Pelham (later 1st Earl of Yarborough)* [verso] c.1785

Watercolour on ivory, octagonal, 7.6cm (3in) high
Provenance: by family descent
PRIVATE COLLECTION

This memorable portrait bears on the verso a portrait by Cosway of the son of the sitter, Charles Anderson-Pelham, later 1st Earl of Yarborough (1781–1846), riding a hobby-horse. Skirving unsuccessfully tried to emulate Cosway during his stay in London during the late 1770s and early 1780s.

John Donaldson 1737–1801

39 *Unknown Lady* 1787

Watercolour on ivory, oval, 4cm (1⅝in) high
Signed and dated on recto: J.D. / 1787
Provenance: NGS; transferred in 1982
Literature: Foskett 1987, p.530; Smailes 1990, p.352
SCOTTISH NATIONAL PORTRAIT GALLERY

Born in Edinburgh, Donaldson worked in London and exhibited his delicately painted miniatures there between 1761 and 1791.

Pompeo Batoni 1708–87

40 *James Bruce of Kinnaird* 1762

Oil on canvas, 72.4 × 62.2cm (28½ × 24½in)
Provenance: bequeathed by Lady Ruthven in 1885
Literature: Smailes 1990, pp.44 and 47, ill.
SCOTTISH NATIONAL PORTRAIT GALLERY

Pompeo Batoni was the leading portrait painter in Rome when Skirving arrived there in 1787. Batoni painted the famous African explorer James Bruce (1730–94) in Rome in 1762.

John Runciman 1744–68

41 *Self-portrait* 1767–8

Oil on panel, 68.7. × 55.6cm (27 × 21⅞in)
Signed on verso: *John Runciman / Seipse Pinxit / A.D. 1767*; inscribed on verso: *To Mr. Robert Allan / Sun Fire Office / Edinr.*
Provenance: thought to have been acquired by the artist's maid after his death; probably acquired by Alexander Runciman; David Laing; Society of Antiquaries of Scotland; on loan since 1882
Literature: Smailes 1990, pp.250–51, ill.
Exhibited: Liverpool 1994–5, p.85, no.32, ill.; London and Rome 1996–7, p.66, no.25, col. pl.
SOCIETY OF ANTIQUARIES OF SCOTLAND, EDINBURGH [ON LOAN TO THE SCOTTISH NATIONAL PORTRAIT GALLERY]

This self-portrait by the young Scottish artist John Runciman was painted during his three-year visit to Italy, where he died. In its device of a hat casting a shadow this portrait bears formal comparison with Skirving's *Self-portrait* [61], drawn in Rome during 1790. Skirving may have known John Runciman's self-portrait, when it probably belonged to his brother, Alexander, after the latter's return from Rome to Edinburgh in 1771.

Archibald Skirving

42 *Adam Skirving* c.1770

[colour plate 1]
Oil on canvas, 76.2 × 60.9cm (30 × 24in)
Provenance: by family descent to David Ainslie; bequeathed by him in 1901
Literature: Smailes 1990, pp.266–7
SCOTTISH NATIONAL PORTRAIT GALLERY

There is another autograph version of this portrait [fig.2] in the Art Gallery of New South Wales, Sydney, presented by R.C. Scot Skirving in 1956. He also gave that gallery the artist's companion portrait of his step-mother *Christian Carnegie, Mrs Adam Skirving* [fig.3], and an early *Self-portrait*, painted just before this date [fig.5]. A family tradition as-

serted that this self-portrait had been painted by 'Revillon', which is likely to be a corruption of the name of Charles Pavillon, a Frenchman who was Master of the Trustees' Academy in Edinburgh from 1768 to 1772. Archibald Skirving may have studied there (Free 1981 and 1987, pp.178–9; Scot Skirving 1988, pp.22–4).

Pietro Fabris fl.1768–78

43 *Kenneth Mackenzie, Viscount Fortrose (later 1st Earl of Seaforth) at Home in Naples: Fencing Scene* 1771

Oil on panel, 35.5 × 47.6cm (14 × 18¾in)
Signed and dated on verso: *P. Fabris p.1771*
Provenance: by descent from Lord Fortrose's daughter, Caroline, Comtesse de Melfort; purchased in France by Jocelyn Fielding Fine Art Ltd, London; purchased with the assistance of the National Art Collections Fund in 1984
Exhibited: London 1996, pp.128–9, col. pl.
Literature: Smailes 1990, pp.337 and 339, ill.
SCOTTISH NATIONAL PORTRAIT GALLERY

Lord Fortrose (1744–81) also commissioned a pair to this scene from Fabris [44].

Pietro Fabris fl.1768–78

44 *Kenneth Mackenzie, Viscount Fortrose (later 1st Earl of Seaforth) at Home in Naples: Concert Party* 1771

Oil on panel, 35.5 × 47.6cm (14 × 18¾in)
Signed and dated on verso: *P. Fabris p.1771*
Provenance: by descent from Lord Fortrose's daughter, Caroline, Comtesse de Melfort; purchased in France by Jocelyn Fielding Fine Art Ltd, London; purchased with the assistance of the National Art Collections Fund in 1984
Exhibited: London 1996, pp.128–9, col. pl.
Literature: Burlington Magazine 1996, pp.128–9, col. pl.; Smailes 1990, pp.337 and 339, ill.
SCOTTISH NATIONAL PORTRAIT GALLERY

The artist has included himself working on the painting in the extreme left foreground. Among the musicians are Mozart and his father playing on keyboards in the left background, while the seated figure playing the viola to the left of the central group is Sir William Hamilton [80], the British envoy in Naples, who was also a patron of Fabris (Brown 1996, pp.39–43). Hamilton was also depicted by Skirving in 1790, in an untraced portrait, for which he was paid the considerable sum of 200 guineas.

Franciszek Smuglevicz 1745–1807

45 *James Byres of Tonley and Members of his Family* c.1775–8

Oil on canvas, 63.2 × 75.8cm (24⅞ × 29⅞in)
Provenance: Christie's, London, 15 July 1983, lot 66; purchased with the assistance of the National Art Collections Fund in 1983
Literature: Ford 1984, pp.111–15; Smailes 1990, pp.337 and 340, ill.
SCOTTISH NATIONAL PORTRAIT GALLERY

James Byres (1733–1817) was a leading Scottish art dealer and antiquarian in Rome, whom Skirving would have known well during his stay there. Byres is the second figure from the left. On the extreme left is his younger sister Isabella Byres, Mrs Robert Sandilands (b.1737). The other figures are, left to right, his father, Patrick Byres of Tonley (1713–78), his mother, Janet Moir (1711–87) and Christopher Norton (d.1799). A similar group portrait is in the collection of Sir Brinsley Ford (*Walpole Society* 1998, I, pl.77, II, p.55).

Attributed to David Allan 1744–96

46 *Alexander Fraser Tytler, later Lord Woodhouselee* 1778

[fig.21]
Oil on canvas, 91.4 × 66.1cm (36 × 26in)
Inscribed on recto: *Alex: Fraser Tytler / at Woodhouselee / 1778*
Provenance: by family descent
PRIVATE COLLECTION

Alexander Fraser Tytler was a distinguished Edinburgh lawyer and historian, who was later elevated to the bench as Lord Woodhouselee. In 1798 he was drawn meticulously in crayons by Skirving [91], and six years later was painted more broadly in oils by Raeburn [142, fig.20]. In this portrait he is depicted in a conversation piece format, seated in the library of Woodhouselee, the family home near the Pentland hills to the south of Edinburgh. This portrait can be compared to David Allan's conversation piece in oils from 1783 of *Three Connoisseurs: John Caw (d.1784), John Bonar (1747–1807) and James Bruce* in an interior (National Gallery of Scotland, Edinburgh). Like Skirving, David Allan studied in Rome (1767–77).

Ascribed to David Allan 1744–96

47 *James Craig c.1780*

[fig.8]

Oil on canvas, 76.7 × 60.8cm (30¼ × 24in)
Provenance: RSA; presented in 1910; on loan to
Huntly House Museum, Edinburgh
SCOTTISH NATIONAL PORTRAIT GALLERY

James Craig (1744–95) devised the layout
of Edinburgh's New Town, the plan for
which can be seen in Thomas Kitchin's
engraved *Plan of Edinburgh* published in
1772 [52]. This portrait probably belonged
to Skirving, as it is almost certainly the
painting described in the artist's studio
in 1819. William Bruce valued the picture,
'supposed Mr Craig', at 7s 6d. [168], while
George Watson valued the same portrait
(no.23), 'A full length Painting of a Architect supposed Craig supposed by D.
Allan', at £26 5s. [169].

Angelica Kauffman 1741–1807

48 *Sir James Hall of Dunglass 1785*

Oil on canvas, 60.5 × 49.5cm (23⅞ × 19½in)
Inscribed on verso: *Rome. 1785 / January / For
Sir James Hall / English Chevalier. Portrait of
the above. Life size head on canvas / not
including hands, paid for / on 20th February 24
Zecchini*
Provenance: by family descent to Mrs E.K.M.
Jackson; purchased in 1995
Literature: NACF *Review* 1995, p.171, col. pl.
SCOTTISH NATIONAL PORTRAIT GALLERY

James Hall of Dunglass (1761–1832) was
an eminent geologist and chemist. This
portrait was painted by Kauffman in
Rome, during the sitter's three year
Grand Tour (1783–6). Angelica Kauffman
was an immensely fashionable history
painter and portraitist in oils.

Hugh Douglas Hamilton c.1739–1808

49 *Prince Charles Edward Stewart
c.1785–6*

Oil on canvas, 25.7 × 22cm (10⅛ × 8⅝in)
Provenance: Dowell's, Edinburgh, 24 October
1903; purchased
Literature: Cullen 1984, pp.200–201; Smailes
1990, pp.277 and 279, ill.; London 1996–7,
pp.164–5, ill.
SCOTTISH NATIONAL PORTRAIT GALLERY

This portrait of Prince Charles Edward
Stewart (1720–88) was painted in Rome
during the last few years of the sitter's
life. At this time Hamilton also portrayed

the Young Pretender's daughter, Charlotte Stewart, Duchess of Albany in a
similar format [50]. The Prince was also
portrayed in pastel in 1748 by Maurice-
Quentin de La Tour [1], while in exile in
Paris. The Irish artist Hugh Douglas
Hamilton is the likely cause of Skirving's
transformation as a crayon painter during the early years of his stay in Rome in
the late 1780s. This canvas still has its
original frame (London 1996–7, p.164). A
similar pastel of this portrait, together
with a pendant of the sitter's younger
brother, Prince Henry Benedict, survives
in a Scottish private collection. Other oil
versions are in the Dundee City Art Gallery and the National Portrait Gallery,
London.

Hugh Douglas Hamilton c.1739–1808

50 *Charlotte Stewart, Duchess of
Albany c.1785–8*

Oil on canvas, 25.7 × 22cm (10⅛ × 8⅛in)
Provenance: Dowell's, Edinburgh, 24 October
1903; purchased through the Gray bequest
Literature: Cullen 1984, p.180; Smailes 1990,
pp.15 and 17, ill.
SCOTTISH NATIONAL PORTRAIT GALLERY

Charlotte Stewart, Duchess of Albany
(1753–89) was the daughter of Prince
Charles Edward Stewart and Clementina
Walkinshaw. The Prince was also portrayed at this time in a similar format by
Hugh Douglas Hamilton [49]. Skirving is
likely to have been aware of Hamilton's
work in pastel while he was in Rome. This
canvas is an autograph copy after an
earlier pastel at Waddesdon Manor,
National Trust (cf. Cullen 1984, pl.72).

Alexander Nasmyth 1758–1840

51 *Robert Burns 1787*

[fig.30]

Oil on panel, 38.4 × 32.4cm (24 × 17½in)
Signed on verso: *Painted from / Mr Robert
Burns by / his friend Alex. Nasmyth / Edinb.
1787*
Provenance: bequeathed by Colonel Williams
Burns in 1872
Literature: Smailes 1990, pp.50–51, ill.
SCOTTISH NATIONAL PORTRAIT GALLERY

Nasmyth's famous portrait of Burns was
copied by Skirving in his equally well-
known 'keel', or red chalk, drawing [103],
which was drawn after the poet's death.

Thomas Kitchin

52 *Plan of the City, Castle and Suburbs
of Edinburgh 1772*

Line engraving (cut down), 35.8 × 47.6cm
(14⅛ × 18¾in)
Titled: *Plan of the* CITY, CASTLE *and Suburbs of
Edinburgh, 1772. / Engraved by Thos. Kitchin /
Hydrographer to His* MAJESTY / MDCCLXXIII
Exhibited: Edinburgh and London 1997–8,
p.30, col. fig.30
SCOTTISH NATIONAL PORTRAIT GALLERY

This city plan of Edinburgh was part of a
much larger map of *The Counties of
Haddington, Edinburgh & Linlithgow; …
Map of the Three Lothians*, which was
dedicated in 1773 to the local nobility,
gentry and clergy by the publishers,
Andrew and Mostyn Armstrong. Copies
of the larger map belong to the City of
Edinburgh Central Library and to the
East Lothian Council Museums Service,
Haddington.

John Raphael Smith 1752–1812 after
Jean-Étienne Liotard 1702–89

53 *The Right Hon. John Stuart,
Viscount Mountstuart 1774*

Mezzotint engraving, 45.7 × 35.6cm (18 × 14in)
Lettered: *Painted by Liotard / Publish'd 30th.
May 1774, by J.R. Smith No.4 Exeter Court
Strand / Engraved by J.R. Smith. / The Right
Honble. John Lord Viscount Mountstuart / Lord
Lieut. & Custos Rotulorum of the County of*
GLAMORGAN
SCOTTISH NATIONAL PORTRAIT GALLERY

John Stuart, Viscount Mountstuart
(1744–1814), later 4th Earl and 1st Mar-
quis of Bute, was the eldest son and heir
of John, 3rd Earl of Bute. The original
pastel by Liotard, which was commissioned by the sitter's father and drawn at
Geneva in 1763, survives in a private
collection, as does a head and shoulders
version by the artist (Loche &
Roethlisberger 1978, p.112, no.260 and
col. pl.49). A preparatory drawing is in
the Musée d'art et d'histoire, Geneva
(Geneva and Paris 1992, pp.234–5, no.127,
col. pl.). Liotard, who was born in Geneva, and who travelled across Europe
and the Near East in the course of his
long career, was one of the finest pastellists of the 18th century. He made two
visits to London, the first from 1753 to
1755 and a second from 1773 to 1774. It was

during the latter visit that his ambitious pastel, which had been drawn a few years earlier, was exhibited at the Royal Academy and this mezzotint published. Skirving's pastel portraiture from the 1790s and the early 1800s can be compared with Liotard's, especially in its use of plain backgrounds, shallow depth of field and simple observation and characterisation.

John Kay 1742–1826

54 *Citizen Skirving* 1794
Photograph of etching
Lettered: *I. Kay fecit 1794 / CITIZEN SKIRVING / Secretary to the British Convention – / A Tried Patriot and an Honest Man. –*
Literature: Clune 1969, opp. p.32, ill.; Scot Skirving 1988, p.26, ill.
CENTRAL LIBRARY, CITY OF EDINBURGH COUNCIL

This was the frontispiece to *The Trial of William Skirving* [57], published in Edinburgh in 1794. John Kay was the leading caricaturist working in Edinburgh during Archibald Skirving's lifetime (cf. Evans & Evans 1973). He also produced portrait miniatures and small oils.

S.I. Neale & Son

55 *Map of Haddington* 1822
Coloured engraving (folded in four), 48.6 × 67cm (19⅛ × 26⅓in)
CENTRAL LIBRARY, CITY OF EDINBURGH COUNCIL

In this map of East Lothian, published three years after Skirving's death in 1819, many of the places the artist knew throughout his life can be identified in the vicinity of the market town of Haddington: the farm at East Garleton where he was born and brought up; the nearby village of Althelstaneford where he was buried; and the Wemyss estates at Amisfield and Gosford, owned by a local landowning family with whom the Skirvings were closely associated. This map was the second plan in the *Atlas of Scotland* produced by the Edinburgh firm of John Thomson & Co.

Adam Skirving 1719–1803

56 *Elegy on the Laird of Congalton*
Printed broadsheet
Provenance: David Laing Papers
UNIVERSITY OF EDINBURGH LIBRARY

This is an example of the poems composed by the artist's father, a habit which Archibald Skirving continued. Congalton is a village in East Lothian.

William Skirving d.1796

57 *The Trial of William Skirving* 1794
Lettered: *The Trial of William Skirving, Secretary to the British Convention; before the High Court of Justiciary, on the 6th and 7th of January, 1794; for Sedition. Containing a full and circumstantial account of all the proceedings and speeches, as taken down in short-hand, by Mr Ramsey, short-hand writer, from London. Edinburgh, printed, and sold for William Skirving, by James Robertson, printer and bookseller, no.4. Horse Wynd, Edinburgh 1794*
Printed book, octavo, 1st edn
Provenance: Michael Phillips; Christopher Edwards
PRIVATE COLLECTION

William 'Citizen' Skirving was one of the five famous Scottish 'martyrs' – political radicals – who were tried for sedition in Edinburgh in a series of notorious trials and transported to Botany Bay in 1793 and 1794 (cf. Skirving 1836). The other radicals were William Gerrald, Maurice Margarot, Thomas Muir, and the Revd Thomas Fyshe Palmer (Clune 1969). They suffered a traumatic voyage to Australia. A monument to the martyrs in the form of an obelisk was erected in 1844 at the Old Calton burial ground in Edinburgh. This edition of William Skirving's trial is missing the etched frontispiece portrait by John Kay of *Citizen Skirving* [54]. The exact relationship between William and Archibald Skirving, who were both born into farming families, has yet to be defined. At the time of the trial Archibald Skirving was in Italy, while during William Skirving's brutal transportation in 1795, the artist was suffering greatly in Brest prison, his boat returning from Italy having been captured by the French. Simultaneously, it was Archibald Skirving's own sympathies for the French Revolution, testified to in Venice, which helped to secure his release from appalling conditions in prison during 1795 (Montaiglon & Guiffrey, 1887–1912, XVI, p.385).

James Hogg 1770–1835

58 *The Jacobite Relics of Scotland; being the Songs, Airs and Legends, of the Adherents to the House of Stuart*, Edinburgh 1821
Printed book, octavo
CENTRAL LIBRARY, CITY OF EDINBURGH COUNCIL

This collection of songs is opened at the famous Jacobite ballad 'Hey, Johnnie Cope', about events surrounding the battle of Prestonpans in 1745, the words to which were composed by the artist's father, Adam Skirving. In a note about this song, Hogg, the noted poet also known as 'The Ettrick Shepherd', referred to Archibald Skirving as 'whimsical'.

Unknown Artist

59 *Standard of William Keith, 3rd Earl Marischal* early 16th century
Cloth, 45.7 × 142.3cm (18 × 56in)
Embroidered on recto: VERITAS VINCIT
Provenance: William Keith, 3rd Earl Marischal; 'Black' John Skirving of Plewlandhill; by family descent to William Skirving; presented by him in 1808
Literature: Balfour Paul 1918, pp.52–4
THE FACULTY OF ADVOCATES, EDINBURGH

Little survives from the earlier history of the Skirving family, who were farmers in East Lothian. However, at the battle of Flodden Field in 1513, this banderol of William Keith, 3rd Earl Marischal of Scotland, was carried by his standard-bearer, 'Black' John Skirving of Plewlandhill. When his descendant William Skirving presented it to the Faculty of Advocates in Edinburgh in 1808, it was accompanied by a letter. This explained that, according to family tradition, after the disastrous battle, 'Black' John Skirving was taken prisoner but had been able to wrap the banner around his body. The motto and the heraldic badges of the three harts' heads are those of the Earl Marischal family.

Archibald Skirving

60 *Gavin Hamilton* 1788–9

[colour plate 6]
Pastel, 61 × 48.7cm (24 × 19³/₁₆in)
Engraved in line by Robert Scott in 1793
Provenance: Skirving's studio until 1819;
Mrs Leila Hoskins; presented by her in 1981
Exhibited: Edinburgh 1993, p.25, col. pl.12
Literature: NLS, MS 10102.a-b; Smailes 1990,
pp.135 and 137, ill.
SCOTTISH NATIONAL PORTRAIT GALLERY

Skirving's memorable and supremely
frank pastel portrait of the history
painter and archaeologist Gavin Hamilton (1723–98) was drawn in Rome, almost
certainly in 1788–9. In the early part of
1788, Francis Garden, Lord Gardenstone,
as recorded in his *Travelling Memorandums*, commissioned from Skirving 'a
miniature painting of the worthy and
ingenious painter Mr Gavin Hamilton'
(Gardenstone 1802, III, pp.152–3). Although the miniature is untraced, the
composition is known from an engraving
by Robert Scott [79], as well as from this
pastel. (The engraving was published in
the 1793 edition of the Edinburgh periodical *The Bee*.) It is unclear as to
whether the miniature or this pastel was
created first, although it was probably
the latter. The pastel is listed in William
Bruce's 1819 valuation of Skirving's
studio contents at 10s 6d., and at 100
guineas in George Watson's valuation
from the same year, making it the single
most expensive item in his list. Hamilton
was also drawn more conventionally in
the previous decade – in 1777 – by Ozias
Humphry [7] (Lloyd Williams 1994,
frontispiece).

Archibald Skirving

61 *Self-portrait* 1790

[front cover]
Pastel, 71.4 × 54.9cm (28⅛ × 21⅝in)
Provenance: Patrick Murray of Simprim in
1790; Miss Ainslie in 1863; by family descent to
David Ainslie; bequeathed by him in 1901
Exhibited: Edinburgh 1863, no.321; Edinburgh
1955, p.13, no.75; Edinburgh 1993, p.90
Literature: NLS, Laing Papers, La.IV.25;
Smailes 1990, pp.266–7
SCOTTISH NATIONAL PORTRAIT GALLERY

This self-portrait was drawn in Rome and
completed by 1790. It is first recorded as
belonging to Patrick Murray of Simprim,
near Forfar, who was the illegitimate son
of the 5th Baron Elibank. He was in Rome
in 1790 with his tutor, the Revd Daniel
Robertson. Skirving portrayed both men,
probably in pastels, and the pictures –
since untraced – were also in Murray's
collection in 1790. This self-portrait is
very likely to be the drawn head 'of himself', which is noted in the list of 'pictures
under glass' in George Watson's 1819
valuation of Skirving's studio contents
[169].

Archibald Skirving

62 *Francis Charteris, Viscount Elcho of Amisfield* 1790

[colour plate 7]
Pastel, 58.4 × 47cm (23 × 18½in)
Provenance: by family descent
Literature: Skinner 1970, p.47
THE RT HON. THE EARL OF WEMYSS
& MARCH, KT

Lord Elcho MP (1749–1808) was the eldest
son of the Hon. Francis Charteris of
Amisfield (1725–1808), who in 1787 became 7th Earl of Wemyss [23, 30, fig.4].
He and his son, Francis Charteris (1772–
1853) [63], visited Rome in 1790, when
they were both portrayed in pastel by
Skirving. This portrait is mentioned by
the artist in a letter written on 18 December 1790 and sent to his brother Robert in
India (Skinner 1970, p.47). The pastel was
later used as the basis for a posthumous
full-length portrait of Lord Elcho by
Raeburn (Wemyss collection, Stanway
House). In a letter from Lord Elcho to
Robert Skirving, the artist's brother in
India, written from Rome on 6 January
1790, the sitter remarked on Archibald's
high reputation and how he intended to
make efforts to further his career (Skinner 1970, p.47).

Archibald Skirving

63 *Francis Charteris, 8th Earl of Wemyss and 4th Earl of March* 1790

Pastel, 58.4 × 47cm (23 × 18½in)
Provenance: by family descent
THE RT HON. THE EARL OF WEMYSS
& MARCH, KT

The sitter was the son of Francis
Charteris, Viscount Elcho of Amisfield
(1749–1808) [23, 30, fig.4] whom he accompanied on a tour of Italy in 1790
(Ingamells 1997, p.334). It was during
their visit to Rome that this pastel of the
eighteen-year-old Francis Charteris was
drawn by Skirving. The 8th Earl of
Wemyss (1772–1853) was also portrayed by
Raeburn (Wemyss collection, Gosford
House). The 8th Earl's daughters received lessons in drawing from Skirving
(Smiles 1862, II, p.278).

Archibald Skirving

64 *Hugh Cleghorn of Stravithie* 1790

[fig.10]
Pastel, 61 × 50.8cm (24 × 20in)
Cartouche on recto inscribed: *Hugh Cleghorn,*
LLD / *of Stravithie* / *d.1836*
Provenance: by family descent
Literature: Skinner 1970, p.47; Clark 1992, ill.
frontispiece
PRIVATE COLLECTION

This pastel of the academic, diplomat
and traveller Hugh Cleghorn of Stravithie
(1752–1837), who was professor of history
at St Andrews University, was drawn by
Skirving in Rome during the sitter's six
months' stay in the city from late 1789,
while acting as bear-leader (or guide) to
Alexander Home, 10th Earl of Home [65,
fig.11] (Ingamells 1997, p.214). In a letter
of 18 December 1790, written by the artist
to his brother Robert in India, Skirving
mentions that he has finished a portrait
of 'a Mr Cleghorn from St Andrew's'
(Skinner 1970, p.47).

Hugh Douglas Hamilton *c*.1739–1808

65 *Alexander Home, 10th Earl of Home* 1790

[fig.11]
Pastel, fictive oval, 25.8 × 21cm (10¼ × 8¼in)
Signed and dated on recto: *H Hamilton / fect.*
Rome / 1790; inscribed in pen and ink on verso:
*Alexander Earl of Home / born 11 Novr. 1769 /
died 21 Oct 1841 / Rome 1790*
Provenance: by family descent
THE RT HON. THE EARL OF HOME CVO, CBE

This pastel of Alexander Home, 10th Earl of Home (1769–1841) was drawn in Rome during the sitter's Grand Tour. His guide was Hugh Cleghorn of Stravithie (Ingamells 1997, p.515), who was drawn in pastel by Skirving at about the same time [64, fig.10]. These connections are evidence of the closeness of Skirving and Hamilton. An unfinished version of this pastel belongs to the same private collection.

Archibald Skirving

66 Father James McCormick c.1787–94

[fig.14]
Red chalk, 37.5 × 27.5cm (14¾ × 10¾in)
Inscribed by the artist and signed on recto:
Father James McCormick / an Irish Franciscan Friar . Professor of Divinity at the College of St. Isidore / AS
Provenance: Mrs Leila Hoskins; her sale, Christie's & Edmiston's, Glasgow, 9 April 1981, lot 23 (part)
Literature: Sundström 1994
ANDREW SKIRVING

This is one of the few informal but finished portrait studies drawn by Skirving while in Rome. It can be compared to the *Unknown Family in Rome* of 1792 [76 and frontispiece].

Archibald Skirving

67 A Landscape with Three Stags c.1787–94

Black chalk, 21.7 × 16.8cm (8½ × 6⅝in)
Inscribed on recto in pencil with initials: *A.S.*
Provenance: presented by Miss Bruce of Edinburgh in 1938
Literature: Andrews & Brotchie 1960, p.219
NATIONAL GALLERY OF SCOTLAND

This landscape is likely to be one of the series of such drawings that Skirving made during his stay in Rome from 1787 to 1794 [68–75].

Archibald Skirving

68 An Entrance to a Park c.1787–94

[fig.13]
Pencil, 27.8 × 19.9cm (10⅞ × 7⅞in)
Inscribed on recto in pencil with initials: *A.S.*
Provenance: presented by Miss Bruce of Edinburgh in 1938
Exhibited: Edinburgh 1993, p.90
Literature: Andrews & Brotchie 1960, p.219
NATIONAL GALLERY OF SCOTLAND

This drawing is one of the more finished examples of Skirving's landscape studies made during his stay in Rome [67, 69–75].

Archibald Skirving

69 Donkey and Foal c.1787–94

Red chalk, 17.2 × 19.7cm (6⅝ × 7¾in)
Provenance: presented by Miss Bruce of Edinburgh in 1938
Literature: Andrews & Brotchie 1960, p.219
NATIONAL GALLERY OF SCOTLAND

On grounds of medium, technique and format, this study is likely to have been drawn during the artist's visit to Rome.

Archibald Skirving

70 A Canopy Suspended from a Tree c.1787–94

Red chalk, 27.9 × 19.6cm (11 × 7⅝in)
Provenance: presented by Miss Bruce of Edinburgh in 1938
Literature: Andrews & Brotchie 1960, p.220
NATIONAL GALLERY OF SCOTLAND

This is one of the surviving group of red chalk drawings made by Skirving during his stay in Rome [67–9, 71–5].

Archibald Skirving

71 The Dome of St Peter's Basilica, Rome c.1787–94

Red chalk, 23.2 × 18.8cm (9⅛ × 7⅜in)
Provenance: presented by Miss Bruce of Edinburgh in 1938
Literature: Andrews & Brotchie 1960, p.220
NATIONAL GALLERY OF SCOTLAND

This is one of Skirving's landscape drawings made in Rome [67–70, 72–5].

Archibald Skirving

72 A Gate in the Gardens at the Back of St Peter's, Rome c.1787–94

Red chalk, 19 × 25.7cm (7⅜ × 10⅛in)
Inscribed by artist on verso in red chalk:
A Gate in the Gardens, Back of St Peter's. 4 A [deleted] P.M.
Provenance: presented by Miss Bruce of Edinburgh in 1938
Literature: Andrews & Brotchie 1960, p.220
NATIONAL GALLERY OF SCOTLAND

This is one of Skirving's three surviving red chalk drawings that include the dome of St Peter's [71, 73].

Archibald Skirving

73 A Villa with the Dome of St Peter's, Rome, in the Background c.1787–94

Red chalk, 27.4 × 19.7cm (10¾ × 7¾in)
Inscribed on recto in pencil: *A.S.*
Provenance: presented by Miss Bruce of Edinburgh in 1938
Literature: Andrews & Brotchie 1960, p.220
NATIONAL GALLERY OF SCOTLAND

This is one of the three red chalk studies that include the dome of St Peter's [71–2].

Archibald Skirving

74 The Basilica of San Paolo fuori le Mura, Rome c.1787–94

Red chalk, 19 × 26cm (7½ × 10¼in)
Inscribed by artist on recto in red chalk:
St. Paul's 6PM and 4
Provenance: presented by Miss Bruce of Edinburgh in 1938
Literature: Andrews & Brotchie 1960, p.220
NATIONAL GALLERY OF SCOTLAND

This red chalk study is one of the landscape drawings made by Skirving during his stay in Rome [68–73, 75].

Archibald Skirving

75 The Fontana dei Cavalli Marini in the Borghese Gardens, Rome c.1791–4

Red chalk, 20 × 27.7cm (7¾ × 10¾in)
Provenance: presented by Miss Bruce of Edinburgh in 1938
Literature: Andrews & Brotchie 1960, p.220
NATIONAL GALLERY OF SCOTLAND

Skirving must have created this drawing after 1791, the date by which the fountain of sea-horses, designed by Cristoforo (or Christoph) Unterberger, was completed (information from Margaret Mackay).

Archibald Skirving

76 An Unknown Family in Rome 1792

[frontispiece]
Pencil, 35.2 × 24.2cm (14 × 9½in)
Signed and dated on recto: *Skirving / Rome 1792*
Provenance: Edward Barrett; Sotheby's, London, 23 November 1920, lot 197; bought by Paul Oppé; by family descent
Literature: Skinner 1959, pp.43–4; Laing 1974, p.348, ill.
Exhibited: Sheffield 1952, no.55; Norwich 1958, no.51; Rome 1959, no.581, pl.66; London 1974, no.18; Edinburgh 1966, no.17; London 1968, no.51; London and Rome, 1996–7, no.55
PRIVATE COLLECTION

The identity of this family on the Grand Tour is unknown. However, they are most likely to be Scottish. It is known that Skirving met the family of the banker Sir William Forbes (1739–1806), 6th Baronet of Pitsligo [82], who was in Rome for a week at the end of 1792 (NLS, Forbes MS Journal). Forbes was accompanied by his wife, Elizabeth Hay, and one of their children, a girl (Winchester, Hampshire Record Office, Robert Parker, MS 'Journal of a Tour into Italy' [1792–3], 18 M51/555). This drawing prefigures Ingres's portrait drawings of British and other visitors to Rome, made between 1806 and 1820. By depicting a family, it anticipates the social change in the pattern of visits to Italy, ranging from the young male aristocrats' Grand Tour during the 18th century, to the rise of family-oriented tourism in the 19th century (Laing 1974).

Archibald Skirving

77 *Four Studies from the Plaster Cast of a Leg* 1793

[fig.12]
Red and black chalk, 24.3 × 35.6cm (9⅝ × 14in)
Signed and dated on recto: *Rome 5th April 1793*; inscribed on recto: *before b / Archd – Skirving*
Provenance: presented by Mrs Leila Hoskins in 1973
NATIONAL GALLERY OF SCOTLAND

This drawing is the only surviving study by Skirving from the great number of drawings of sculpture that he made in Rome. Portfolios of these are listed in the 1819 inventories of his studio contents (NLS, MS 10102.a-b). One early commentator noted that the artist 'brought back from Italy many drawings and sketches – some in black chalk – of statues and garden scenery, very highly finished – and others in crayons of statues in the Vatican' (Cleghorn 1848, II, p.205).

Unknown Italian Etcher after Jacob More 1740–93

78 *Self-portrait* after 1783

Hand-coloured etching, 28.4 × 18.5cm (11⅛ × 7¼in)
Lettered: *Jacopo More Pitt. Paesista / nato in Edimburgo Capitale della Scozia nel 1740. Vive in Roma / 229*
SCOTTISH NATIONAL PORTRAIT GALLERY

The Scottish artist Jacob More was one of the leading landscapists resident in Rome, where he stayed for the last twenty years of his life (Holloway 1987). Skirving would have known him during his stay in Rome. Sir William Forbes of Pitsligo [82] invited the two artists to dinner on 7 May 1793 (NLS, Forbes MS Journal). Skirving also wrote of More's death in a letter of 5 March 1794 to George Cumberland, the London-based art critic (London, British Library, Cumberland MS 36497, ff.290–

91). This etching is after More's ambitious *Self-portrait* in the Galleria degli Uffizi, Florence, painted in 1783 (cf. London and Rome 1996–7 [Rome only], pp.67–8, no.26, col. pl.).

Robert Scott 1771–1841 after Archibald Skirving

79 *Gavin Hamilton* 1793

Stipple engraving, 15.2 × 10.2cm (6 × 4in)
Lettered: *Skirving Pinx: / R. Scott sculp. / GAVIN HAMILTON. / Painter. / Published by J Anderson July 10th 1793*
SCOTTISH NATIONAL PORTRAIT GALLERY

This engraving was published in 1793 while Skirving was still in Rome. It is after his untraced miniature portrait of Gavin Hamilton (1723–98), the eminent Scottish artist and archaeologist, who spent most of the last forty years of his life in Rome.

James Tassie 1735–99

80 *Sir William Hamilton* 1784

Paste medallion, oval, 7.3cm (2⅞in) high
Inscribed on base: s w HAMILTON / *Tassie F. 1784*
Provenance: purchased in 1885
Literature: Gray 1894, p.113, no.177; Smailes 1990, pp.138–9, ill.
SCOTTISH NATIONAL PORTRAIT GALLERY

Skirving made an untraced portrait of Sir William Hamilton (1730–1803), the collector, archaeologist and diplomat, in his night-cap and dressing gown, for which the artist was paid the considerable sum of 200 guineas. A portrait of Hamilton similar to the Tassie medallion was made by Wedgwood and Bentley at Etruria in 1779 (London 1996, p.160, no.37, col. pl.).

James Tassie 1735–99

81 *Allan Maconochie, 1st Lord Meadowbank* 1791

Paste medallion, oval, 7.4cm (2⅞in) high
Inscribed on base: *Tassie F /* ALLAN MACONOCHIE / *1791*
Provenance: presented by the descendants of the Revd Alexander Bryce in 1887
Literature: Smailes 1990, p.205
SCOTTISH NATIONAL PORTRAIT GALLERY

The Scottish judge Lord Meadowbank (1748–1816) was portrayed by Skirving before 1802 (cf. Skinner 1970, p.55; and NLS, MS 10102.c).

James Tassie 1735–99

82 *Sir William Forbes of Pitsligo* 1791

Paste medallion, oval, 8cm (3¹⁄₁₆in) high
Engraved on base of medallion: SIR WILL. FORBES / OF PITSLIGO BARONET / *1791 /* TASSIE F.
Provenance: purchased in 1889
Literature: Gray 1894, p.103, no.128; Smailes 1990, p.131
SCOTTISH NATIONAL PORTRAIT GALLERY

The banker and author Sir William Forbes (1739–1806), 6th Baronet of Pitsligo, visited Italy with his wife and one of his younger daughters in 1792–3. He noted in his manuscript journal that he met Skirving on a number of occasions, describing him as 'a very ingenious artist' who took such a time over his portrait commissions that he 'can scarcely live by his art'. A profile portrait by Skirving of Forbes was engraved in stipple by T. Woolnoth (O'Donoghue & Hake, II, p.234).

James Tassie 1735–99 after Sir Henry Raeburn 1756–1823

83 *Sir Henry Raeburn* 1792

Paste medallion, oval, 7.6cm (3in) high
Inscribed on base: *H. Raeburn / 1792*
Provenance: W. Carlisle Baillie; purchased in 1922
Exhibited: Edinburgh and London 1997–8, p.82, no.16, col. pl.
Literature: Gray 1894, p.138, no.317; Smailes 1990, pp.240–41, ill.; Liverpool 1994–5, p.80, no.27, ill.
SCOTTISH NATIONAL PORTRAIT GALLERY

Another cast of this portrait in the National Gallery of Scotland (NG 1959) bears an old inscription on the verso: 'Presented to Adam Smith by his much esteem'd friend Henry Raeburn Author of this medal 1792' (Liverpool 1994–5, p.80, no.27, ill.). This medallion is after the only portrait sculpture known to have been made by Raeburn. He was well known for making toy boats, just as Skirving delighted in making furniture and bone egg-cups.

Archibald Skirving

**84 *Robert Boswell of St Boswells
c.1795–6***

[colour plate 10]
Pastel, 81.3 × 64.8cm (32 × 25½in)
Lithographed by N. Chater & Co. after a
drawing copied from the pastel by P. Ronan
[165]
Provenance: by family descent
Exhibited: London 1956–7, p.205, no.677
Literature: Simon 1987, p.95, fig.195;
Sundström 1994
PRIVATE COLLECTION

Robert Boswell (1746–1804) was the first
cousin of the famous biographer James
Boswell (1740–95) and law agent for the
executry of the latter's estate (Buchanan
1975, p.28). The sitter's feelings towards
his brilliant but dissolute cousin are
evident from the words of the epitaph he
composed for him: 'Bury his failings in
the silent grave / And from unfriendly
hands his memory save'. Son of John
Boswell, President of the Royal College of
Physicians in Edinburgh, Robert
Boswell was made a Writer to the Signet
in 1773, and was appointed interim Lord
Lyon King of Arms in 1795–6. One of the
most respected lawyers in Edinburgh,
for nearly thirty years, up until 1800, he
was Clerk to the Royal College of Physicians. In 1769 he married Sibella, daughter of William Sandeman of Luncarty
and a merchant in Perth. They had fourteen children and forty-two grandchil-
dren. A deeply religious man, he was a
Glasite, and was married by the founder
of that evangelical sect, the Revd John
Glas. His father-in-law William
Sandeman succeeded John Glas as leader
of this group, which stressed the rever-
ent power of silence and abhorred the
vanity of words. In later life he and his
family retired to live in St Boswells. He
died suddenly of heart disease while
preaching in a Glasite meeting house in
London. An oil version of this powerful
portrait is in a private collection. In the
upper left of the pastel can be seen part
of another portrait, which may well
represent an otherwise unrecorded
portrait of Robert Boswell wearing his
heraldic uniform of tabard and crown.

Archibald Skirving

**85 *Janet Skirving, Mrs James Carnegie
of Edrom Newton c.1796–1803***

[colour plate 9]
Pastel, 60.3 × 45cm (23¾ × 17¾in)
Provenance: the artist's studio in 1819;
bequeathed by James Carnegie in 1899
Exhibited: Edinburgh 1863, no.336 ('collection
of James Carnegy [sic] Esq.')
Literature: NLS, MS 10102.a-b; NGS 1980, p.135, ill.
NATIONAL GALLERY OF SCOTLAND

Janet (Jessy) Skirving (1772–1853) was the
artist's half-sister by his father's second
wife, Christian Carnegie. Despite her
plain appearance, Skirving lavished unremitting attention on her portrayal. In his
1819 valuation of Skirving's studio,
William Bruce listed a framed and glazed
pastel portrait of 'Mrs Carnegie, at Hails'
(£1 1s 6d.).

Archibald Skirving after Henri-Pierre
Danloux 1753–1809

**86 *Mary Drummond, Mrs John Pringle
of Stitchell c.1798***

[colour plate 11]
Pastel on paper, 63.5 × 47.6cm (25 × 18¾in)
Inscribed in pen and ink on verso: *Mary
Drummond b. 17th- Decr- 1719 / 6th- daur- of
James 2nd- Laird of Blair Drummond, m. John
Pringle / W.S. of the family of Stitchell, in /
crayons by Scirving [sic] – she d. 9 April / 1804.–*
Provenance: by family descent
Literature: Edinburgh, Scottish Record Office,
MS, Inventory of Blair Drummond House (post–
1825), GD24/1/346/7(10)
PRIVATE COLLECTION

Mary Drummond (1719–1804) was the
sixth daughter of James Drummond, 2nd
Laird of Blair Drummond (1673-1739) and
Jean Carre of Cavers (1681-1766). She
married John Pringle of Stitchell, who was
a Writer to the Signet. In the late 1790s
Skirving also drew in crayons a portrait of
another member of the family, Henry
Home Drummond, 6th Laird of Blair
Drummond (1783–1867) [87]. The portrait
of *Mary Drummond* is referred to in an
inventory – drawn up after 1825 (water-
mark) – of the contents of Blair
Drummond House, hanging in the small
drawing room: 'done in crayons by
Skirving from an original by Danloux and
at one sitting of Mrs Pringle'. The original
oil by Danloux is untraced.

Archibald Skirving

**87 *Henry Home Drummond, 6th Laird
of Blair Drummond c.1798***

[colour plate 12]
Pastel, 59.8 × 44.4.cm (23½ × 17½in)
Inscribed in pen and ink on verso: *Henry
Home / Drummond. 6th- Laird of / Blair
Drummond b. / 28. July 1783 – in crayon /
by Skirving. -*
Provenance: by family descent
Literature: Edinburgh, Scottish Record Office,
MS, Inventory of Blair Drummond House (post–
1825), GD24/1/346/7(10), Small Drawing Room
('A Portrait in Crayons by Skirving of Henry
Home Drummond of Blair Drummond')
PRIVATE COLLECTION

This pastel was presumably commissioned from Skirving either by the sitter's
father, George Home Drummond
(d.1819), 5th Laird of Blair Drummond,
or by his mother, Janet Jardine (d.1840).
Both were portrayed in 1798 (private
collection) by Henri-Pierre Danloux, the
French *émigré* artist, who worked inter-
mittently in Scotland between 1796 and
1800. Henry Home Drummond, 6th
Laird of Blair Drummond (1783–1867)
later became Deputy-Lieutenant and MP
for Perthshire. In 1812 he married Christian, daughter of Charles Moray of
Abercairny. The landscape background in
the pastel is thought to represent a scene
on the Blair Drummond estate. At about
this date Skirving also produced a pastel
of another member of the sitter's family,
Mary Drummond, Mrs John Pringle of
Stitchell (1719–1804) [86], which he had
copied from an untraced oil portrait by
Danloux.

Archibald Skirving

**88 *Mrs Johnston of Hutton Hall
c.1796–1800***

[colour plate 13]
Pastel, 62.7 × 50.9cm (24⅝ × 20in)
Provenance: bequeathed by Miss E.K.H. Scott
in 1939
Exhibited: Edinburgh 1993, p.90
Literature: NGS 1980, p.135, ill.
NATIONAL GALLERY OF SCOTLAND

Little is known about Mrs Johnston of
Hutton Hall in Berwickshire. This pastel
of a fashionably dressed sitter is perhaps
the artist's most exuberant portrait.

Archibald Skirving

**89 William Craig, Lord Craig
c.1796–1801**

[colour plate 8]
Pastel, 68.8 × 55.9cm (27¹/₁₆ × 22in)
Engraved in mezzotint by George Dawe in 1801
[149]
Provenance: Maxwell of Dargavel family; by
descent to Sir Edward Playfair; presented after
long-term loan in 1996
Literature: Smailes 1990, pp.75 and 76, ill.;
Burlington Magazine 1997, p.582, ill.
SCOTTISH NATIONAL PORTRAIT GALLERY

This sensitively drawn pastel of the Scottish judge Lord Craig (1745-1813) is one of
Skirving's series of portraits of legal
figures – such as *Robert Boswell of St
Boswells* [84] and *Alexander Fraser
Tytler, Lord Woodhouselee* [91] – that
were made in Edinburgh around the turn
of the century. Born in Glasgow, the sitter
studied at Edinburgh University and was
called to the bar in 1768. A man of wide
literary interests, he was a member of the
society known as 'The Tabernacle', and it
was at his suggestion that they started the
periodical, *The Mirror*, which lasted for
eighteen months. Craig and Henry Mackenzie were its most regular contributors.
'The Tabernacle' later became 'The Mirror' club, and between 1785 and 1787 they
published another periodical called 'The
Lounger'. The sitter was raised to the
bench in 1794, and in the following year
was appointed a judge of the Court of
Justiciary. Despite Lord Cockburn's
scathing criticism of Craig, he was known
both publicly and privately for his up-
right conduct and courteous manners.
This is likely to be the original frame.

Archibald Skirving

**90 Margaret Sym, Mrs John Wilson
c.1797–1800**

[colour plate 14]
Pastel, 68.5 × 56cm (27 × 22in)
Provenance: by family descent; presented by
Miss Marjorie A. Wilson in 1984
Exhibited: Edinburgh 1990, p.33, no.29
Literature: *Burlington Magazine* 1985, fig.100;
Smailes 1990, pp.309 and 311, ill.
SCOTTISH NATIONAL PORTRAIT GALLERY

This pastel of Margaret Sym, Mrs John
Wilson (1753-1824), is one of Skirving's
masterpieces in this medium, particularly notable for the sensitivity in the
depiction of appearance and character,
as well as the details of dress and cap.

Despite having a glass eye, the sitter was
considered to be one of the most striking
women of her generation in Paisley, where
she grew up. She later married John
Wilson (1734-97), a successful gauze
manufacturer in the town. One of their
children was the noted author and moral
philosopher Professor John Wilson (*nom
de plume* 'Christopher North'). She was
remembered as one of the 'old school of
Scottish ladies, whose refinement and
intellect never interfered with duties the
most humble'. Of stately bearing, she was
often seen elegantly wearing a black satin
dress. Skirving has shown Mrs Wilson
wearing black, in mourning after the death
of her husband. The pastel is set in its
original neo-classical frame, almost certainly chosen by the artist.

Archibald Skirving

**91 Alexander Fraser Tytler, Lord
Woodhouselee 1798**

[colour plate 15]
Pastel, 69.8 × 57.2cm (27½ × 22½in)
Provenance: Mr G.M. Fraser Tytler, Edinburgh,
in 1880; the Trustees of Skene Tytler Estate,
Keith Marischal (formerly on loan to the
SNPG [PGL 214]); Commander Christopher
Hallewell; purchased from him in 1957 by the
present owner
Exhibited: Edinburgh 1880, no.412; Edinburgh
1955, p.14, no.79
Literature: Sundström 1994
LADY ERSKINE

The sitter was an Edinburgh lawyer and
historian. Born Alexander Tytler (1747-
1813), on his marriage in 1776 to Ann
Fraser, he changed his name to Fraser
Tytler. In 1780 he was appointed joint
professor of Universal History at the University of Edinburgh, occupying the chair
in his own right from 1786. He was described by Lord Cockburn as 'a person of
correct taste'; however, there was 'no
kindness in insinuating that he was a man
of genius, and of public or even social
influence, or in describing Woodhouselee
[his estate by the Pentland Hills to the
south of Edinburgh] as Tusculum'. He was
appointed judge-advocate of Scotland in
1790, and raised to the bench as Lord
Woodhouselee in 1802.

The sittings to Skirving occurred in
1798 as is known from a postscript to a
letter of 26 July from Lord Woodhouselee's
daughter Anne and son James to their
aunt, Miss Tytler in Stirling: 'I forgot to

tell you Papa is sitting to Mr. Skirving for
his picture; and though it has not got an
eye in its head yet, will probably turn out
a very good portrait. At present it is truly
formidable. I wish you were here to see it'
(Laing 1914-25, II, pp.659-61).

This pastel of Lord Woodhouselee is
still in its original frame. In 1804
Raeburn portrayed Lord Woodhouselee
and his wife in head and shoulder portraits, which are in a private collection
[142, fig.20] and the Brooklyn Museum of
Art, New York (Edinburgh and London
1997-8, pp.124-5, no.35), respectively.

Archibald Skirving

92 John Clerk of Eldin 1799–1800

[colour plate 16]
Pastel, 58.7 × 49.2cm (23⅛ × 19⅜in)
Signed and dated at upper right: *A. Skirving
1800*
Engraved in mezzotint by Samuel William
Reynolds in 1801 [148]
Provenance: by family descent
Exhibited: London 1799, no.836; Edinburgh
1981, p.14, no.16; Edinburgh and London 1986-
7, p.136, fig.61 and p.196, no.118
Literature: Graves 1905-6, VII, p.117; McIntyre
& McKirdy 1997, p.v, col. pl.
ADAM COLLECTION

John Clerk of Eldin (1728–1812) was a
geologist and naval theorist, as well as a
gifted and original amateur etcher, who
may well have been taught by Paul
Sandby during one of his visits to Scotland during the 1770s. A son of Sir John
Clerk of Penicuik, he was the father of
John Clerk, Lord Eldin (1757-1832), and
younger brother of Sir John Clerk of
Penicuik (d.1798), the subjects of well-
known portraits by Sir Henry Raeburn in
the Scottish National Portrait Gallery and
the National Gallery of Ireland respectively. Clerk's celebrated treatise on
Naval Tactics was highly influential,
being used by Nelson and also indirectly
leading to the development of Patrick
Miller's steamship. He was a friend of
James Hutton, the founding father of
geology as a science, and accompanied
him on many of his expeditions across
Scotland. This pastel, which was exhibited at the Royal Academy in London in
1799, was the only one of Skirving's works
in crayons shown there. He had previously exhibited a frame of three miniatures in 1779.

Archibald Skirving

93 *Benjamin Yule of Wheatfield*
c.1796–1800

[fig.16]
Pastel, 28.5 × 25.3cm (11¼ × 10in)
Provenance: by family descent
Literature: Tancred 1903, pp.456–7; Sundström
1994
PRIVATE COLLECTION

Benjamin Yule of Wheatfield (b.1740), a
royal baxter (baker) in Edinburgh, was
the son of Benjamin Yule, a burgess of the
city. The sitter married Marion Sprot
(1750–1808/12) [94], who was the sister of
Mark Sprot (1743–1808), the financier
[140, 145]. Mark Sprot and his wife,
Joanna Stewart of Physgill, were also
portrayed by Skirving [see 146]. The
Yules, who had four daughters, were
buried in St Cuthbert's churchyard in
Edinburgh. This, and the following, are
the two smallest pastel portraits by
Skirving to have survived.

Archibald Skirving

94 *Marion Sprot, Mrs Benjamin Yule*
of Wheatfield c.1796–1800

[fig.17]
Pastel, 28.5 × 25.3cm (11¼ × 10in)
Provenance: by family descent
Literature: Tancred 1903, pp.456–7; Sundström
1994
PRIVATE COLLECTION

Marion Sprot (1750–1808/12) was a
daughter of Janet Espline and John Sprot
(1703–79) of Edinburgh. Her brother was
Mark Sprot (1743–1808), a financier. He
and his wife were also portrayed by
Skirving [145–6].

Archibald Skirving

95 *Robert Dundas of Arniston*
1800–1801

[colour plate 17]
Pastel, 106.1 × 65.4cm (41¾ × 25¾in)
Provenance: by family descent
THE DUNDAS-BEKKER FAMILY, ARNISTON
HOUSE

One of Skirving's largest pastels, still in
its original frame and glass, and his only
known full-length in crayons, this portrait of Robert Dundas of Arniston (1797–
1838) was drawn when he was three or
four. The young boy is shown wearing a
dress, which was commonplace until the
age of five. There does not appear to be
any family significance in the fact that the

boy holds an owl. The owl may have been
injured or a tame pet, or even a stuffed
toy. The background shows the Moorfoot
Hills, which mark the southern end of the
Arniston estate. The sitter was the eldest
son of Robert Dundas of Arniston (1758–
1819), a judge and Chief Baron of the
Exchequer in Scotland. He travelled to
south-eastern Europe in 1818, and after
returning to Scotland, became Advocate-
Depute in 1822 (Omond 1887). An elder
cousin was the all-powerful politician
Henry Dundas, 1st Viscount Melville
(1742–1811), whose oil portrait by David
Martin was probably copied in pastel by
Skirving [4, fig.6].

Archibald Skirving

96 *Margaret Cussans Grant, Mrs*
William Fraser Tytler c.1801

Pastel, 62.2 × 54cm (24½ × 21¼in)
Provenance: by family descent
Literature: Sundström 1994
LADY ERSKINE

Margaret Cussans Grant (d.1862) was the
daughter of George Grant of Burdyards in
Morayshire. In 1801 she married William
Fraser Tytler, the eldest son of Lord
Woodhouselee who had been painted in
crayons by Skirving in 1798 [91]. This
pastel of Margaret Cussans Grant was
most likely drawn at the time of her marriage. Margaret bore William five sons
and five daughters.

Archibald Skirving

97 *Isabella Fraser Tytler c.1801*

Pastel, 62.4 × 54cm (24½ × 21½in)
Provenance: J.S. Fraser Tytler in 1880; by family
descent
Exhibited: Edinburgh 1880, no.427
Literature: Baile de Lapperiere 1991, IV, p.174
THE SIR HENRY WADE TRUST

Isabella Fraser Tytler (1784–1841) was the
second daughter of Lord Woodhouselee,
who had been painted in crayons by
Skirving in 1798 [91]. Her portrait probably dates to the same year as Skirving's
pastel of her sister-in-law, *Margaret*
Cussans Grant, Mrs William Fraser
Tytler [96]. Isabella was painted by her
eldest sister Anne in a scene of her family
in the dining-room at their home of
Woodhouselee near Edinburgh [111].
This pastel of Isabella Fraser Tytler, who
died unmarried, is in its original frame.

Archibald Skirving

98 *Lady Charlotte Campbell c.1802*

[fig.18]
Pastel, 45.7 × 38.1cm (18 × 15in)
Provenance: Skirving's studio in 1819; Capt.
Wilkie (in 1863); Mrs Leila Hoskins; Sotheby's,
London, 22 March 1979, lot 137 [size:
67.5 × 54.5cm (26½ × 21½in)], sold in joint lot
with paired portrait of Colonel John Campbell of
Shawfield; Christie's, Edinburgh, 15 May 1997,
lot 578 (cut down to present size)
Exhibited: Edinburgh 1863, no.352 (shown with
Col. John Campbell, no.331, also belonging to
Capt. Wilkie)
Literature: NLS, MS 10102.a-b; Cleghorn 1848, II,
p.204; Carlyle 1974, p.133, n.14
THE FINE ART SOCIETY, LONDON

Lady Charlotte Susan Campbell (1775–
1861) was a daughter of John, 5th Duke of
Argyll and sister of George, the 6th Duke.
An authoress, she married Colonel John
Campbell of Shawfield, who was also drawn
in pastels by Skirving, a profile portrait
reportedly destroyed in the early 1980s
(information from Simon Edsor). Their
son Walter Frederick Campbell of
Shawfield, MP for Argyll, married Eleanor,
eldest daughter of Francis, 8th Earl of
Wemyss. Lady Campbell's portrait was left
unfinished by Skirving, because of his
refusal to complete the work. Her dis-
tracted behaviour during the sittings led to
the artist issuing an ultimatum to Lady
Campbell, which was a serious breach of
decorum (Cleghorn 1848; Carlyle 1974).
This unfinished pastel – and that of her
husband – remained in the artist's studio
until his death. In his valuation the painter
George Watson noted the value of the pair,
including seventeen years worth of interest, at £106 4s. Earlier in Lady Campbell's
life, during a visit to Naples in 1789, she
was painted in an unusually composed full-
length oil portrait by the German artist
Johann Heinrich Wilhelm Tischbein (Scottish National Portrait Gallery, PG 2275),
whom Skirving had met in Italy.

Archibald Skirving

99 *An Unknown Lady 1803*

[colour plate 18]
Pastel on vellum, 72.4 × 59.6cm (28½ × 23½in)
Signed and dated lower right: *A. Skirving 1803*
Provenance: H.W. Cage Esq., 1901; Esmé
Church; Messrs Clifford Dann & Partners,
Lewes, Sussex, 15–16 April 1980, lot 172;
McEwan Gallery, Ballater
Literature: Sundström 1994
PRIVATE COLLECTION

This three-quarter length portrait of an old lady has been erroneously identified as the Countess of Hopetoun. The pastel, which still has its original frame, has recently been conserved, and is unique in the artist's *oeuvre* for being drawn on vellum. A copy is known to have been painted by Skirving as a rectangular portrait miniature (Foskett 1987, p.236, pl.57c). Formerly in a private collection and currently untraced, this copy was attributed to the Irish miniaturist John Comerford (c.1770–1832). Also in 1803, Skirving drew a signed and dated – but untraced – pastel of Susan Campbell, Mrs Craufurd Tait of Harviestoun (d.1814), daughter of Sir Ilay Campbell and mother of Archibald Campbell Tait (1811–92), later Archbishop of Canterbury (Lyon & Turnbull, Edinburgh, 4 November 1950, lot 91).

Archibald Skirving and an Unknown Artist

100 *Maria Cuninghame of Lainshaw (later Maria Edmonstoune-Cranstoun of Corehouse) c.1800–1805*

[fig.19]
Pastel, 68.6 × 55.8cm (27 × 22in)
Provenance: Skirving's studio in 1819; collected by Mr Cranstoun; by family descent
Literature: NLS, MS 10102.b; Sundström 1994.
PRIVATE COLLECTION

This pastel portrait of Miss Maria Cuninghame of Lainshaw (d.1863) was recorded in the artist's studio by George Watson in 1819 as being unfinished, with a note added that it had been collected by Mr Cranstoun, a relative of the sitter. He valued it at £35. It can be surmised that only the head and background were completed by the artist, and that the dress was added during the 1830s by an unknown pastellist (information from Rosalind Marshall). Maria Cuninghame, who, on inheriting the Corehouse estate from her maternal uncle, changed her name to Edmonstoune-Cranstoun, died unmarried.

Archibald Skirving

101 *Patrick Sheriff of Mungoswells c.1796–1800*

[fig.24]
Red chalk, 35.6 × 28.9cm (14 × 11⅜in)
Inscribed on recto in pen and ink: *Mr. Sheriff*; on verso in pencil: *portrait of Patk Sheriff of Mungowells* [sic]. *East Lothian / drawing by Archd Skirving / 1749–1819*
Provenance: presented by Miss Bruce of Edinburgh in 1938
Literature: Andrews & Brotchie 1960, p.219
NATIONAL GALLERY OF SCOTLAND

This informal portrait study is of a member of the Sheriff family, who were neighbours of the Skirvings. The farm of Mungoswells is about a mile north of East Garleton farm, near Haddington, where the artist was born and brought up.

Archibald Skirving

102 *An Unknown Gentleman c.1796–1800*

Pencil, irregular, 14.2 × 12.4cm (4⅜ × 3⅜in)
Provenance: presented by Miss Bruce of Edinburgh in 1938
Literature: Andrews & Brotchie 1960, p.220
NATIONAL GALLERY OF SCOTLAND

This unfinished oval profile drawing is a unique survival of Skirving's small scale studies for his portraiture, and may be related to a miniature.

Archibald Skirving after Alexander Nasmyth 1758–1840

103 *Robert Burns 1796–8*

[colour plate 19]
Red chalk, 54.9 × 42.5cm (21⅝ × 16¾in)
Engraved in line by John Beugo c.1796–8 [147]; lithographed by William Holl [166]
Provenance: Skirving's studio in 1819; George Rennie; by family descent; Sir Theodore Martin; purchased in 1911
Selected Exhibitions: Edinburgh 1863, no.393; Edinburgh and Kilmarnock 1996
Selected Literature: NLS, MS 10102.a-c; Skinner 1959, p.43, ill; Skinner 1970, p.51; Smailes 1990, pp.50–51, ill.; Sprott 1996, p.19, col. pl.
SCOTTISH NATIONAL PORTRAIT GALLERY

This unfinished 'keel', or red chalk, portrait drawing of Robert Burns is by far the most famous work by Skirving, albeit a copy after Alexander Nasmyth's equally well-known *ad vivum* oil on panel portrait [51, fig.30]. In a letter of 17 June 1802 to his brother Robert in India, the artist noted (Skinner 1970, p.51): 'I have been repeatedly offer'd 30 Guineas for a keel-

head of Burns but it is not finished, and [is] still with me. It is taken from a picture (for I never saw him) in the hands of one I despise'. Sir Walter Scott, in a letter of 30 May 1816 to the London-based critic and collector Samuel Rogers, observed that this drawing was 'the only good portrait of Burns'. The drawing is mentioned in 1814 and 1816 in William Chalmers & Son's frame account to Skirving. The portrait was valued in Skirving's studio in 1819 by William Bruce at one guinea and by George Watson at 30 guineas, who also noted that it had been sold to Mr Rennie, presumably the agriculturist brother of the famous engineer, John Rennie. In comparison with Nasmyth's portrait of 1787 and Alexander Reid's miniature of 1795–6 [120], Skirving's portrait – although very finely drawn – is inevitably a somewhat idealised interpretation of the poet. One can only regret that Skirving neither met Burns, nor had the opportunity to draw him from life.

Archibald Skirving

104 *An Unknown Gentleman 1797*

Red chalk, 24 × 21cm (9½ × 8¼in)
Signed and dated on recto: *Skirving / 1797*
Provenance: Mrs Leila Hoskins; her sale, Christie's & Edmiston's, Glasgow, 9 April 1981, lot 23 (part)
Literature: Sundström 1994
ANDREW SKIRVING

This carefully finished profile portrait drawing with its exquisite stippling was completed two years after the artist's return to Edinburgh from Rome in 1795.

Archibald Skirving after William Delacour fl.1747–66

105 *William Berry 1797*

Pencil, 25.7 × 19.2cm (10⅛ × 7⁹⁄₁₆in)
Signed and dated in pencil on recto: *W.D. La Cour Pinxt. 1765 / Skirving D 1797 /* BERRY / *Intagliatore*; inscribed on recto of mount in pen and ink: *William* BERRY, *Engraver of Intaglios, Edinburgh / Born 1730. Died 1783. / Drawn from the Picture of De La Cour by / Archd: Skirving, 1797.*
Provenance: bequeathed by W.F. Watson in 1886
Exhibited: Edinburgh 1812; Edinburgh 1955, no.77
Literature: NLS, MS 10102.a-b; *Scots Magazine*, 1812, p.247; Smailes 1990, p.33; Sundström 1994
SCOTTISH NATIONAL PORTRAIT GALLERY

This drawing of the seal engraver William Berry (1730–83) is a copy by Skirving after an untraced portrait of 1765 by William Delacour, who was active in Scotland during the mid–18th century. In the valuation of Skirving's studio contents in 1819, it was estimated at 5 shillings by William Bruce and 20 guineas by George Watson. It was shown by Skirving in the exhibition of the Society of Artists in Edinburgh during 1812, together with a portrait of Mary Ballingall. The anonymous critic in *The Scots Magazine*, while critical of Skirving's eccentricities, praised 'the great powers of this eminent master'.

Archibald Skirving
106 *Grace Skirving, Mrs Robert Ainslie of Blanesburn c.1796–1800*

Red chalk, 55.8 × 43.2cm (22 × 17in)
Inscribed in pen and ink on verso: ARCHIBALD SKIRVING
Provenance: Miss Ainslie in 1863; by family descent; Mrs A.A. Scot Skirving in 1955; Mrs Leila Hoskins; her sale, Christie's & Edmiston's, Glasgow, 9 April 1981, lot 23 (part)
Exhibited: Edinburgh 1863, no.345; Edinburgh 1955, no.102; Edinburgh and London 1986–7, no.121
Literature: Graves 1913–5, III, p.1228; Baile de Laperriere 1991, IV, p.174
PRIVATE COLLECTION

Grace (or Grizel) Skirving (1760–1848) was sister to the artist. Her husband, Robert Ainslie of Blanesburn, was a farmer in Inveresk, near Musselburgh. It is likely that the artist lived with his sister, who was one of his two executors, during the last three years of his life.

Archibald Skirving
107 *An Unknown Gentleman c.1796–1800*

Red chalk, 26 × 19.5cm (10¼ × 7¾in)
Exhibited: Edinburgh and London 1986–7, no.120
PRIVATE COLLECTION

This sensitive portrait of a young man is an example of Skirving's profile drawings made after his return from Italy and France in 1795 [104, 108–9, 112–13].

Archibald Skirving
108 *An Unknown Gentleman c.1796–1800*

Red chalk, 36.2 × 28.9cm (14⅛ × 11⅜in)
Provenance: by family descent; Mrs A.A. Scot Skirving in 1955
ROBERT SKIRVING HOSKINS

Archibald Skirving
109 *An Unknown Lady c.1796–1800*

Black chalk, 40.7 × 30.8cm (16 × 12⅛in)
Provenance: by family descent
ROBERT SKIRVING HOSKINS

Archibald Skirving
110 *The Hon. Charles Napier of Merchiston 1800*

[fig.25]
White chalk and wash on light mahogany panel, 55 × 45.5cm (22 × 18¾in)
Signed and dated on verso with brush and black wash: *Honble. / Charles Napier / Merchiston Hall / Archd: Skirving / 1800*
Provenance: purchased in 1924
GLASGOW MUSEUMS: ART GALLERY & MUSEUM, KELVINGROVE

This is a unique surviving example of Skirving's drawings in chalk made on wooden panels, which he often used to wipe out after completion. Charles Napier (1731–1807) was son of Francis, 5th Lord Napier of Merchiston. This drawing on mahogany panel has recently been conserved.

Anne Fraser Tytler
111 *The Family of Alexander Fraser Tytler, Lord Woodhouselee, assembled in the Dining-room at Woodhouselee 1804*

Watercolour with pen and ink, 30 × 46cm (11¾ × 18⅛in)
Signed in pen and ink on recto with initials: AFT [and numbers] *1–10* and on verso: *The family of Woodhouselee assembled in the Dining room. September 1804 / 4 Anne Fraser Tytler eldest Daughter of Lord Woodhouselee / 2 Isabella Fraser Tytler his second Daughter / 3 Christina Tytler Sister to Lord Woodhouselee / 1 Jane Fraser Tytler his third Daughter / 5 Patrick Fraser Tytler his fourth son / 6 James Tytler his second son / 7 William Fraser Tytler his eldest son / 8 Anne Fraser Tytler his Wife / 9 Alexr Fraser Tytler his third son / 10 Alex Fraser Tytler L. Woodhouselee*
Provenance: by family descent
Literature: Gow 1996, p.144, col. pl. 144
THE SIR HENRY WADE TRUST

Anne Fraser Tytler, who died unmarried, was the eldest daughter of Lord Woodhouselee, who was drawn in a masterly pastel by Skirving in 1798 [91]. One of her younger sisters, Isabella Fraser Tytler, had been portrayed in crayons by the artist in c.1801 [97], around the time when he had drawn another pastel of one of her sisters-in-law, Margaret Cussans

Grant [96], who married William Fraser Tytler. This accomplished amateur water-colour shows the family of Lord Woodhouselee in the 'gothick' dining-room at the family home of Woodhouselee, near Edinburgh. Anne has depicted herself drawing at a desk, next to the window. The dining-room is being used as an everyday sitting-room, as was customary in Scotland at that time.

Archibald Skirving
112 *An Unknown Lady c.1800–10*

Black chalk, 51.2 × 36.8cm (20⅛ × 14½in)
Provenance: by family descent; Mrs A.A. Scot Skirving in 1955
Exhibited: Edinburgh 1955, no.74
ROBERT SKIRVING HOSKINS

Archibald Skirving
113 *An Unknown Lady c.1805–16*

Pen and wash, 25.2 × 20.3cm (9⅞ × 8in)
Provenance: presented by Miss Bruce of Edinburgh in 1938
Literature: Andrews & Brotchie 1960, p.219
NATIONAL GALLERY OF SCOTLAND

One of Skirving's late profile portrait drawings, this is a unique surviving study of a sitter in pen and wash, the others being in red, black or white chalk.

John Henning 1771–1851
114 *James Watt 1809*

Black chalk, 53 × 43.8cm (20⅞ × 17¼in)
Signed and dated on recto: *Henning F / 1809.*
Provenance: commissioned by Lord Jeffrey; Lady Jeffrey; presented by Miss M. Campbell in 1891
Exhibited: Edinburgh 1810
Literature: Smailes 1990, pp.303 and 305, ill.
SCOTTISH NATIONAL PORTRAIT GALLERY

The profile chalk portrait drawings by John Henning (cf. Paisley and Edinburgh 1977) and Skirving were very close in format and style at this date. This profile of James Watt (1736–1819), the famous engineer and inventor of the steam engine, can be compared to the shared portrait by the two artists of *Professor Dugald Stewart* [115]. The friendship between Henning and Skirving was marked by the former modelling a porcelain portrait medallion of the latter in 1811.

John Henning 1771–1851 and Archibald Skirving

115 *Professor Dugald Stewart c.1810–19*

Black chalk, 49.5 × 41.9cm (19½ × 16½in)
Inscribed in pen and ink on verso: *Dugald Stewart / by / Skirving / from the Collection of the late Carnegie Esqre- W.S. / Edinburgh*
Provenance: James Carnegie in 1863; R.K. Miller; on loan since 1885
Exhibited: Edinburgh 1863, no.392
Literature: NLS, MS 10102.c; Smailes 1990, pp.279–80, ill.

R.K. MILLER [ON LOAN TO THE SCOTTISH NATIONAL PORTRAIT GALLERY]

This profile is likely to be that listed in Bruce's 1819 valuation of Skirving's pictures, a glazed and framed portrait of 'Professor Dugald Stewart suppsd: finished by Mr S', which was valued at 20 guineas. A similar portrait by Henning belongs to the National Portrait Gallery, London. The philosopher Dugald Stewart (1755–1828) was a brilliant teacher, who succeeded in 1785 to the chair of Moral Philosophy at Edinburgh University. He was largely responsible for raising the intellectual reputation of Edinburgh at this period.

Archibald Skirving

116 *A. Handasyde Esq.* 1816

Red chalk, 45.7 × 33.1cm (18 × 13in)
Signed and dated on recto: *London 30th: June / 1816* AS */ La Sorella / Di quello / e bella / A: Handasyde*; inscribed in pen and ink on verso: *Arch [Skirv]ing / A Crayon Head / Jas Carnegie Esq*
Provenance: James Carnegie; R. Scot Skirving in 1883; by family descent; Mrs A.A. Scot Skirving in 1955
Exhibited: Edinburgh 1883, no.467; Edinburgh 1955, no.76
Literature: Sundström 1994

ROBERT SKIRVING HOSKINS

This profile drawing is one of a few made by Skirving during his last visit to London in 1816.

Archibald Skirving

117 *An Unknown Lady* 1816

Red chalk, 50.8 × 36.7cm (20 × 14½in)
Signed in monogram and dated on recto: *London July / 1816* AS
Provenance: by family descent
Literature: Sundström 1994

ELISABETH A. McINTYRE

This sensitively drawn profile portrait of an elderly sitter, which has suffered from damp-staining, was drawn by Skirving during his visit to London in 1816. The drawing is in its original frame which was almost certainly made in Edinburgh by William Chalmers & Son.

Philip Jean 1755–1802

118 *Elizabeth Bradshaigh Dalrymple, Countess of Balcarres and Crawford c.1793*

Watercolour on ivory, oval, 6.7cm (2⅝in) high
Provenance: by family descent

PRIVATE COLLECTION

Elizabeth Bradshaigh Dalrymple married her first cousin Alexander, 6th Earl of Balcarres and 23rd Earl of Crawford (1752–1829) in 1780. This miniature may have been painted in 1793, when the sitter's husband was Civil Governor and Commander-in-Chief of Jersey. Philip Jean was born in Jersey and served in the Navy as a young man. He exhibited his miniatures at the Royal Academy from 1787 until his death. His style is varied and shows the influence of a number of leading miniaturists of the period, including Jeremiah Meyer and Richard Cosway. This is a notably fine example of his work, and its fluent brushwork and forthright pose invite comparison with Skirving's miniatures from the later 1790s, such as the *Unknown Gentleman* [122] and the *Unknown Officer* [123].

François Ferrière 1752–1839

119 *Major-General John Ramsay* 1794

Oil on ivory, oval, 8cm (3⅛in) high
Signed and dated on verso: *F. Ferrière pt / 1794*
Provenance: purchased in 1946
Exhibited: Edinburgh 1965, no.280
Literature: Smailes 1990, pp.241–2, ill.

SCOTTISH NATIONAL PORTRAIT GALLERY

The soldier John Ramsay (1768–1845) was son of Allan Ramsay the artist [2]. François Ferrière was born in Geneva and studied in Paris. He moved to Britain in 1793, exhibiting miniatures in London until 1804, when he travelled to St Petersburg. He came back to Britain in 1817, exhibiting his strongly characterised portrait miniatures for five years before returning to Geneva. He included a number of Scots among his clientele.

Alexander Reid 1747–1823

120 *Robert Burns* 1796

Watercolour on ivory, rectangular, 7.6cm (3in) high
Autograph pasted on recto: *Burns*; engraved coat of arms on verso with lettering: *John Mitchell Dumfries Sapiens Qui Assiduus*
Provenance: bequeathed by W.F. Watson in 1892
Exhibited (most recently): Edinburgh and Kilmarnock 1996
Selected Literature: Smailes 1990, pp.50–51, ill.; Sprott 1996, p.18, col. pl.

SCOTTISH NATIONAL PORTRAIT GALLERY

This miniature is considered by many to be the most lifelike portrait of Burns (1759–96), who sat to the artist in January 1796, the year of his death. It can be compared to Skirving's slightly later idealised 'keel' portrait drawing [103] after Alexander Nasmyth's earlier *ad vivum* oil on panel [51, fig.30]. Alexander Reid worked in Dumfries and painted oil portraits, landscapes and miniatures.

Attributed to Archibald Skirving

121 *Charles Philippe, Comte d'Artois (later Charles X)* 1796–7

Watercolour on ivory, oval, 8.1cm (3⅛in) high, set onto lid of gold and ebonised snuff-box, circular, 9cm (3½in) dia.
Provenance: gift of Louis Antoine, Duc d'Angoulême to Mr Manners
Exhibited: Edinburgh 1951, p.33, no.131

PRIVATE COLLECTION

According to a letter – kept inside this snuff-box – dated 27 March 1797, and sent from Edinburgh by Louis Antoine, Duc d'Angoulême (1775–1844) to a Mr Manners, the box with the inset miniature was a present from 'Louis Antoine', as he signed the accompanying letter. He was the elder son of the sitter, the Comte d'Artois (1757–1836), who was a younger brother of Louis XVI. Charles Philippe ascended the French throne in 1824 – after the death of his brother Louis XVIII – and reigned as Charles X until his abdication in 1830. During the French Revolution the family were exiled at the Palace of Holyroodhouse in Edinburgh, the Comte d'Artois staying there from 1796 until at least 1803 (Mackenzie-Stuart 1995). The sitter was known as 'Monsieur' and he acclimatised well to life in Edinburgh. The accompanying letter indicates that the miniature was most likely painted in 1796–7. Skirving had only just returned to

Edinburgh after his traumatic journey back from Italy. The attribution to Skirving of this ambitious miniature, confidently painted with diagonal strokes in the background and with full, open-mouthed characterisation (the sitter's mouth was permanently open!) that betrays a knowledge of Richard Cosway's recent work in London, is supported by comparison with the confident handling of Skirving's contemporaneous signed miniatures of an *Unknown Officer* [123] and an *Unknown Gentleman* from 1798 [122]. The Comte d'Artois was also portrayed in Edinburgh during 1796 in oils by the French *émigré*, Henri-Pierre Danloux (1753–1809). A reduced replica of that portrait, dated 1797, is in the collection of the Duke of Buccleuch at Bowhill (Smailes 1985, pp.38–9).

Archibald Skirving
122 *An Unknown Gentleman* **1798**
Watercolour on ivory, 6.8 cm (2¾ in)
Signed in monogram and dated on recto: AS / *1798*
Provenance: Grossmann; sold by him to Edward Grosvenor Paine in May 1961; Christie's, London, 21 April 1997, lot 188; D.S. Lavender (Antiques) Ltd, London
Literature: Foskett 1972, I, p.511, II, pl.334, no.833; Foskett 1987, p.646
PRIVATE COLLECTION, LONDON

This miniature and the signed miniature of an *Unknown Officer* [123], provide significant evidence for Skirving's activity in this medium in Edinburgh after his return from Italy in 1795. Through stylistic comparison with these two works, the following miniatures can be attributed to Skirving at this period: *Charles Philippe, Comte d'Artois* [121]; *James Drummond, Lord Perth* [124]; and his daughter *The Hon. Clementina Sarah Drummond* [125].

Archibald Skirving
123 *An Unknown Officer c.***1798**
Watercolour on ivory, oval, 7cm (2¾in) high
Signed in monogram on recto: AS
Provenance: Christie's, London, 19 June 1973, lot 95; Phillips, London, 7 November 1994, lot 187
SCOTTISH NATIONAL PORTRAIT GALLERY

This signed miniature, together with the signed and dated miniature of an *Unknown Gentleman* [122] from 1798, form the basis for reconstituting Skirving's *oeuvre* as a miniaturist after his return to Scotland from Italy and France in 1795.

Attributed to Archibald Skirving
124 *James Drummond, Lord Perth* **1798**
Watercolour on ivory, oval, 7.4cm (2⅞in) high
Engraved around gold rim on recto: *James Baron Perth 1798*
Provenance: by family descent
GRIMSTHORPE & DRUMMOND CASTLE TRUST

James Drummond (1744–1800) was granted baronial rank as Lord Perth and Baron Drummond of Stobhall in 1797, the year before this miniature was painted. In 1785 he married the Hon. Clementina Elizabeth, daughter of Charles, 10th Lord Elphinstone. The attribution of the miniature to Skirving can be made because of the stylistic similarities with other miniatures, such as the signed and dated *Unknown Gentleman* [122], also from 1798, and the signed *Unknown Officer* [123]. Also attributed to Skirving from this date is the miniature of Lord and Lady Perth's daughter, Clementina Sarah Drummond [125], later Baroness Willoughby de Eresby.

Attributed to Archibald Skirving
125 *The Hon. Clementina Sarah Drummond (later Baroness Willoughby de Eresby) c.***1798**
[colour plate 5]
Watercolour on ivory, oval, 6.7cm (2⅝in) high
Provenance: by family descent
GRIMSTHORPE & DRUMMOND CASTLE TRUST

Clementina Sarah Drummond (1786–1885) was the daughter and heiress of James Drummond, Lord Perth [124] and of Clementina Elizabeth, daughter of Charles, 10th Lord Elphinstone. The sitter is shown wearing a white dress and blue Highland bonnet with black feather, band with ribbon, bow, streamers and sash of the Drummond tartan. In 1807 Clementina married Peter Robert Burrell, later 2nd Lord Gwydyr and 19th Baron Willoughby de Eresby. Clementina was also painted in a miniature by George Saunders, which can be seen in the background of the cabinet portrait miniature painted by Saunders's niece, Christina Robertson, depicting Clementina's daughters the Hon. Clementina and the Hon. Elizabeth Drummond [135]. This miniature of Clementina can be given the same date as that of her father, on grounds of dress and style. The attribution to Skirving can be made by comparison with other miniatures by the artist,

such as the signed and dated *Unknown Gentleman* [122] from 1798, and the signed *Unknown Officer* [123].

François Ferrière 1752–1839 after Sir Henry Raeburn 1756–1823
126 *James Wauchope of Edmonstone c.***1800–1804**
Watercolour on ivory, oval, 6.6cm (2⅝in) high
Signed and dated indistinctly: *F.F. / 180[-]*
Provenance: NGS; transferred in 1982
Exhibited: Edinburgh 1965, no.279
Literature: Smailes 1990, p.304
SCOTTISH NATIONAL PORTRAIT GALLERY

François Ferrière also painted a miniature of Major-General John Ramsay [119], son of the portraitist. The original oil on canvas portrait by Raeburn of the seated James Wauchope of Edmonstone (1767–97) is in the National Gallery of Scotland (NG 2148).

Unknown Scottish Artist after Sir Henry Raeburn 1756–1823
127 *The Revd John Home c.***1800–1805**
Watercolour on ivory, oval, 7.9cm (3⅞in) high
Provenance: purchased in 1933
Literature: Smailes 1990, p.146
SCOTTISH NATIONAL PORTRAIT GALLERY

The Revd John Home (1722–1808) was a historian and the author of the popular play, *Tragedy of Douglas*. He was minister in Skirving's local village of Athelstaneford in East Lothian from 1747 to 1757.

Andrew Robertson 1777–1845
128 *Unknown Lady* **1807**
Watercolour on ivory, oval, 7.5cm (3in) high
Signed and dated on recto: *A.R. / 1807*
Provenance: NGS; transferred in 1982
Literature: Smailes 1990, p.355
SCOTTISH NATIONAL PORTRAIT GALLERY

The Aberdeen artist Andrew Robertson became the leading miniaturist of his generation and enjoyed great success in London [131, 133].

Alexander Gallaway fl.1794–1812
129 *Mrs Mary Robertson* **1809**
Watercolour on ivory, oval, 7.6cm (3in) high
Engraved on verso: *A. Gallaway / pinxit / Edinburgh 1809*
Provenance: Christie's, London, 7 November 1988, no.118
PRIVATE COLLECTION

The Scottish miniaturist Alexander Gallaway worked in Glasgow and Edinburgh, producing highly realistic and frank portraits. It is known that in 1794 he shared a studio in Glasgow with the landscape watercolourist Hugh William 'Grecian' Williams (1773–1829) (Foskett 1972, I, p.283). On 31 May 1794 the two artists placed an advertisement in the *Glasgow Courier*: *Drawing Academy. / Gallaway and Williams acquaint their friends and the public, that they / have removed their Drawing Academy to 2d. Story of Horn's Court, / Argyll-street, which will open on Monday the 2d. of June.* They also advertised their work on 3 June 1794: *Miniature Painting / By Mr Gallaway, and / Views of Any Particular Place, / Taken from Nature, / By Mr. Williams. / Specimens to be seen at the Academy.* Gallaway exhibited his work in Edinburgh in the 1808 exhibition of the Society of Artists, and it is known that he worked in that city until 1812.

Peter Paillou *c.*1757 – after 1831

130 *An Unknown Gentleman* 1809

Watercolour on ivory, oval, 7cm (2¾in) high
Signed and dated on recto: *P. Paillou 1809*
Provenance: NGS; transferred in 1987
Literature: Smailes 1990, p.355
SCOTTISH NATIONAL PORTRAIT GALLERY

Peter Paillou, junior, came initially from London and exhibited at the Royal Academy from 1786 to 1800. Much of his later career was spent in Scotland. His portraiture is noted for its smoothly painted flesh tones and darkened sky backgrounds.

Andrew Robertson 1777–1845

131 *John Hay Forbes, Lord Medwyn c.*1810

Watercolour on ivory, rectangular, 10.5 × 7.9cm (4¼ × 3⅛in)
Provenance: NGS; transferred in 1982
Literature: Smailes 1990, pp.206–7, ill.
SCOTTISH NATIONAL PORTRAIT GALLERY

The judge Lord Medwyn (1776–1854) was a son of Sir William Forbes of Pitsligo [82].

Unknown Artist after Archibald Skirving

132 *Euphan Guthrie, Mrs Charles Wright of Shallope c.*1796–1810

Watercolour on ivory, oval, 4.2cm (1½in) high
Provenance: by family descent
MAJOR MALCOLM R.S. MACRAE, SKAILL HOUSE, ORKNEY

This finely painted miniature of Euphan Guthrie (1739–1831) was copied from an untraced pastel portrait of the sitter drawn late in Skirving's career (photograph in SNPG archive). The dress has been dated to *c.*1796–1810 (information from Rosalind Marshall).

Andrew Robertson 1777–1845

133 *Self-portrait* 1811

Watercolour on ivory set in octagonal broach, oval, 3.2cm (1¼in) high
Provenance: by family descent; Christie's, London, 12 July 1988, lot 142
Exhibited: Edinburgh 1965, no.328; Edinburgh and London 1995–6, p.129, no.185
SCOTTISH NATIONAL PORTRAIT GALLERY

George Saunders 1774–1846

134 *The Hon. Margaret Mercer Elphinstone (later Baroness Keith and Nairn and Comtesse de Flahault)* 1814

Watercolour on ivory, rectangular, 15.2cm (6in) high
Engraved on verso: *Hon Margaret Marian Elphinstone / Countess de Flahault*
Provenance: by family descent
GRIMSTHORPE & DRUMMOND CASTLE TRUST

The Hon. Margaret Mercer Elphinstone (1788–1867) was the only daughter of the noted admiral Sir George Keith Elphinstone, Viscount Keith [138, fig.22] and his first wife, Jane Mercer. In 1817 the sitter married at Edinburgh Auguste Charles Joseph, the Comte de Flahault de la Billardrie (d.1870), later French ambassador to Vienna. She was portrayed in a similarly exotic Turkish dress in an equally romantic oil painting by Saunders, probably from a year earlier and now in a private collection (Irwin & Irwin 1973, pp.80–81, pl.22). The Scottish portraitist George Saunders (sometimes spelt Sanders) was a significant miniaturist in the late Regency period, who, after starting his career in Edinburgh, moved to London around 1805. This miniature is one of his finest works in this medium.

His niece was Christina Robertson, also a miniaturist, who sometimes worked in oils [135].

Christina Robertson 1796–1854

135 *The Hon. Clementina Elizabeth Drummond (later Lady Aveland) and her sister the Hon. Elizabeth Susan Drummond Willoughby* 1819

Watercolour on ivory, rectangular, 21.5cm (8½in) high
Signed on recto: C. ROBERTSON *1819*; engraved on verso of contemporary gilt-metal frame: *Clementina Elizabeth Lady Aveland / and / The Honble: Elizabeth S Drummond Willoughby / Painted in 1818 when children*
Provenance: by family descent
Exhibited: Edinburgh 1996, p.47, col. ill.
GRIMSTHORPE & DRUMMOND CASTLE TRUST

The two girls depicted – Clementina (1809–88) and Elizabeth (1810–53) – were the daughters of the Hon. Clementina Sarah Drummond, later Baroness Willoughby de Eresby [125], who can be seen in a portrait hanging in the background of this cabinet miniature. Christina Robertson (née Saunders) was the niece of the miniaturist and occasional oil painter George Saunders [see 134]. After beginning her career in Scotland, she exhibited between 1823 and 1849 in London, but later also worked in St Petersburg for the Imperial Court.

Sir William Charles Ross 1794–1860

136 *Anne Isabella Monck, Viscountess Hawarden* 1823

Watercolour on ivory, rectangular, 11.4cm (4½in) high
Inscribed in pen and ink on verso: *Uppr. Charlotte St. / Fitzroy Sqr. / Painted by W.C. Ross / 1823 / Portrait of Isabella, / Dowr. Viscountess Hawarden / No.6*
Provenance: Christie's, London, 16 November 1976, lot 42
Exhibited: Royal Academy, London 1824, no.684
PRIVATE COLLECTION

This miniature of Lady Hawarden is from relatively early in the career of the Scottish artist Sir William Charles Ross. Making his career in London, he became one of the dominant miniaturists in the late Regency and early Victorian periods, and received many commissions from Queen Victoria. Following the example of fellow Scottish artist Andrew Robertson (1777–1845) [128, 131, 133], he mastered the creation of rectangular portrait miniatures that imitated the richness of contemporary oil portraiture.

Kenneth Macleay 1802–78

137 ***Jane Baillie Welsh, Mrs Thomas Carlyle* 1826**

Watercolour on ivory, rectangular, 9.5cm (3¾in) high
Provenance: Alexander Carlyle; presented in 1930
Literature: Smailes 1990, pp.57 and 59, ill.; Smailes 1992, p.6, fig.3
SCOTTISH NATIONAL PORTRAIT GALLERY

Skirving gave drawing lessons to the young Jane Baillie Welsh, the future wife of the historian Thomas Carlyle [152], who wrote the finest memoir on the artist.

Henri-Pierre Danloux 1753–1809

138 ***Admiral Sir George Keith Elphinstone (later Viscount Keith)* 1795–7**

[fig.22]
Oil on canvas, 44.5 × 35.6cm (17½ × 14in)
Provenance: by family descent
Exhibited: Edinburgh 1985, p.50, no.c10, ill.
PRIVATE COLLECTION

This unfinished portrait of Viscount Keith (1746–1823) was a study for Danloux's theatrical full-length oil portrait (The Earl of Shelburne, Bowood House) of the sitter as Vice-Admiral of the Red at the Battle of Muizenberg in 1795, for which the artist asked £600, and which was later engraved.

Danloux was one of the *émigrés* in Britain during the French Revolution. His exile from 1792 to 1802 included a number of visits to Scotland between 1796 and 1800 to undertake commissions, principally at the Palace of Holyroodhouse for members of the exiled French royal family. He was also commissioned by Lord Adam Gordon and Henry, 3rd Duke of Buccleuch. This clearly lit oil study by Danloux, which shows the strong influence of Jacques-Louis David's technique, can be contrasted with Skirving's pastel portraiture from this period. Viscount Keith was the father of the Hon. Margaret Mercer Elphinstone (later Baroness Keith & Nairn and Comtesse de Flahault) who was portrayed in a miniature of 1814 by George Saunders [134].

Henri-Pierre Danloux 1753–1809

139 ***Henry, 3rd Duke of Buccleuch and his Family* 1796–8**

Oil on canvas, 127 × 101.6cm (49½ × 39¼in)
Signed and dated on recto: *HP Danloux f 1798*
Provenance: by family descent
Literature: Steuart 1890, p.81; Portalis 1910, pp.341–4, ill. opp. p.342; Dalkeith House 1911, p.123, no.361; Edinburgh 1985, pp.44–6, ill.
HIS GRACE THE DUKE OF BUCCLEUCH, KT

The French *émigré* portrait painter Danloux was based mainly in London from 1792 to 1802, but made a number of extended visits to Edinburgh between 1796 and 1800. Already an accomplished portraitist in France, working under the influence of Jacques-Louis David, he quickly adapted his style to a British audience, making it slightly less polished than his previous work in France. Apart from working on major full-length portraits of the naval heroes, the Admirals Keith (The Earl of Shelburne, Bowood House) and Duncan (Scottish National Portrait Gallery), he portrayed members of the French royal family in exile at the Palace of Holyroodhouse. However, his major Scottish patron was Henry, 3rd Duke of Buccleuch, who commissioned the artist to portray himself and various members of his family, both in individual small portraits and in this masterly conversation piece of the whole family seen in the park at Dalkeith House, a few miles outside Edinburgh. From left to right the sitters are: Henry James Scott, Lord Montagu; Lady Caroline (later Marchioness of Queensberry); Henry, 3rd Duke of Buccleuch; Lady Elizabeth Montagu, Duchess of Buccleuch; Lady Harriet Scott (later Marchioness of Lothian); Lady Elizabeth Scott (later Countess of Home); the 3rd Earl of Courtown; Harriet, Countess of Dalkeith; Charles, Earl of Dalkeith; and Lady Mary Scott, Lady Courtown. There is a replica of this painting in a Scottish private collection.

Little is known of Skirving's relationship with Danloux, but it is likely that – despite their differing political views over the French Revolution – they would have been well aware of each other's portraits. Both artists were particularly interested in unidealised portraiture, clear and unshadowed lighting, and plain yet sophisticated colour contrast. Skirving may also have painted Danloux in a portrait miniature (Portalis 1910, p.459, ill).

After Archibald Skirving

140 ***Mark Sprot* c.1796–1800**

Oil on panel, 28.5 × 23.5cm (11¼ × 9¼in)
Provenance: by family descent
Literature: Tancred 1903, pp.456–7
PRIVATE COLLECTION

The original pastel portraits of the financier Mark Sprot (1743–1808) and of his wife Joanna Stewart of Physgill (d.1828) are untraced (Tancred 1903, pp.456–7). Mezzotint engravings of the portraits by William Ward exist [145–6]. This copy was probably made in the late 19th century.

Henri-Pierre Danloux 1753–1809

141 ***Lord Adam Gordon* 1799**

Oil on canvas, 27 × 22cm (10⅝ × 8⅝in)
Inscribed and dated on verso: *Lord Adam Gordon / 1799*
Engraved in line by Philip Audinet in 1799
Provenance: James Thomson Gibson Craig; purchased in 1887
Exhibited: Edinburgh 1985, p.42, no.c4, ill.
SCOTTISH NATIONAL PORTRAIT GALLERY

Lord Adam Gordon (c.1726–1801) was a general, governor of Edinburgh Castle and commander of forces in Scotland (1782–98). This unfinished portrait is typical of the preliminary studies that Danloux produced for larger compositions, such as those for the conversation piece of *Henry, 3rd Duke of Buccleuch and his Family* [139]. The portrait of Lord Adam Gordon was copied in a miniature attributed to Miss Annabella Pigott (Phillips, London, 16 July 1986, lot 288, ill.), but which bears a strong stylistic resemblance to Skirving's miniatures painted at this date.

Sir Henry Raeburn 1756–1823

142 ***Alexander Fraser Tytler, Lord Woodhouselee* 1804**

[fig.20]
Oil on canvas, 76.3 × 63.4cm (30 × 25in)
Provenance: by family descent
Literature: Edinburgh and London 1997–8, pp.124–5, no.35
PRIVATE COLLECTION

Painted six years after Skirving's pastel of Lord Woodhouselee [91], this portrait by Raeburn provides an excellent contrast between the two artists' manners in interpreting the same sitter. While Skirving reveals the historian and newly-ennobled judge with unremitting frankness, bathing him in a cool yet clear light, Raeburn –

in one of his lesser works – has the sitter emerge from a darkened background. The sitter is painted far more schematically, with much less attention to detail than in the pastel by Skirving. Two other members of the sitter's family – his father and wife – were painted far more successfully by Raeburn, the atmospheric pre-1790 head and shoulders portrait of *William Tytler of Woodhouselee* (Private Collection) and the highly sensitive portrait from *c.*1804 of Lord Woodhouselee's wife, Anne Fraser Tytler (Brooklyn Museum of Art, New York City).

Archibald Skirving

143 *The Revd Alexander Carlyle c.*1800–1805

Oil on canvas, 76.2 × 63.5cm (30 × 25in)
Provenance: the sitter; Carlyle Bell Esq.; purchased in 1886
Literature: Smailes 1990, p.57
SCOTTISH NATIONAL PORTRAIT GALLERY

This portrait of the divine and pamphleteer, the Revd Alexander Carlyle (1722–1805), is a rare example of Skirving's oil portraiture. It can be compared to his oil, *An Unknown Gentleman, possibly Adam Skirving* [144]. Skirving also drew the sitter in a profile portrait in black chalk, on loan from the Kirk Session of Inveresk to the Scottish National Portrait Gallery (PGL 154). Earlier in his life, Carlyle had been drawn in profile by John Brown (1749–87) [12], and he was painted by Raeburn in 1796, a work also in the Scottish National Portrait Gallery (PG 2724).

Archibald Skirving

144 *An Unknown Gentleman, possibly Adam Skirving c.*1800–10

Oil on canvas, 76.2 × 63.5cm (30 × 25in)
Provenance: Anthony Mould Ltd; purchased in 1997
EAST LOTHIAN COUNCIL MUSEUMS SERVICE

An old cartouche on the frame bore the inscription 'Skirving'. While the elderly sitter has not been identified, it does bear some resemblance to Adam Skirving, the artist's father. In its colouring and tonality the portrait shows the presence of Skirving's hand, especially when compared to the oil, *The Revd Alexander Carlyle* [143]. This canvas has recently been conserved.

William Ward 1766–1826 after Archibald Skirving

145 *Mark Sprot c.*1796–1800

Mezzotint engraving, 33 x 27.3cm (13 x 10in)
Lettered: *A. Scirven* [sic] *Pinxt. / W. Ward Sculpt.*; inscribed in pencil on recto: *Mr. Sprott*
Literature: Chaloner Smith 1878–83, no.77; Frankau 1904, no.275; O'Donoghue & Hake 1908–25, IV, p.169
SCOTTISH NATIONAL PORTRAIT GALLERY

Mark Sprot (1743–1808) – sometimes spelt Sprott – was the son of Janet Espline and John Sprot (1703–79), a deacon of the Guild of Candlemakers in Edinburgh. In early life, aged ten, the sitter had gone to sea. He served in the East India Company and then became a successful financier in the city of London, before retiring in 1775. After his death, he is reputed to have left a fortune of over £100,000, which was intended for his family to buy the estate of Grankirk near Glasgow. Both of Skirving's original portraits of Mark Sprot and his wife Joanna Stewart [146] are untraced (Tancred 1903, pp.456–7), although an oil on panel copy after Skirving's portrait of Mark Sprot exists [140]. The sitter's sister, Marion Sprot, and her husband, Benjamin Yule, were also painted in crayons by Skirving [93–4].

William Ward 1766–1826 after Archibald Skirving

146 *Joanna Stewart of Physgill, Mrs Mark Sprot c.*1796–1800

Mezzotint engraving, 33 × 27.3cm (13 × 10¾in)
Lettered: *A. Scirven* [sic] *Pinxt / W. Ward Sculpt*
Literature: Chaloner Smith 1878–83, no.78; Frankau 1904, no.276; O'Donoghue & Hake 1908–25, IV, p.169
TRUSTEES OF THE BRITISH MUSEUM, LONDON

See the above entry for the paired mezzotint of the sitter's husband *Mark Sprot* [145]. They were married in 1781 and had no children. After her husband's death in London in 1808, Joanna Sprot (d.1828) returned to live in Edinburgh, staying in Abercromby Place.

John Beugo 1759–1841 after Archibald Skirving

147 *Robert Burns c.*1796–8

Line engraving, 17.8 × 10.2cm (7 × 4in)
Lettered: *Nasmyth pinxt / Robert Burns / Engraved from a drawing of A Skirving by J Beugo*
Provenance: bequeathed by W.F. Watson in 1886
SCOTTISH NATIONAL PORTRAIT GALLERY

This is one of the earliest engravings after Skirving's famous red chalk ('keel') portrait drawing of Robert Burns [103], which had been copied (and somewhat idealised) from Alexander Nasmyth's equally well-known *ad vivum* oil on panel portrait of the poet [51 and fig.30].

Samuel William Reynolds 1773–1835 after Archibald Skirving

148 *John Clerk of Eldin, Esqr.* 1800

Mezzotint engraving, 35.6 × 26.1cm (13⅞ × 10¼in)
Lettered: *Painted in Crayons by Skirving. / Engraved by S. W. Reynolds. / John Clerk of Eldin, Esqr. / London, Published Feby. 1. 1800, No.47 Poland Street*
Provenance: bequeathed by W.F. Watson in 1886
Literature: Whitman 1903, p.35, no.56
SCOTTISH NATIONAL PORTRAIT GALLERY

This mezzotint of the naval tactician and draughtsman John Clerk of Eldin (1728–1812) was published in London during 1800, after Skirving's pastel of the sitter [92], which had been previously exhibited at the Royal Academy in 1799.

George Dawe 1781–1829 after
Archibald Skirving

149 *The Hon. William Craig* **1801**

Mezzotint engraving, 44.2 × 35.4cm
(17³⁄₈ × 13⁷⁄₈in)
Lettered: *Engraved by G. Dawe /* THE HONBLE.
WILLIAM CRAIG, / *One of the Senators of the*
College of Justice, and one of the Lord Commis-
sioners of Justiciary for Scotland. / From an
Original Painting by Mr. Skirving. / Published
May 30. 1801. By Alexr. Laurie, Bookseller,
Edinburg [sic].
Provenance: Sanderson bequest to NGS;
transferred
SCOTTISH NATIONAL PORTRAIT GALLERY

This mezzotint by George Dawe is after
Skirving's head and shoulders pastel of
the Scottish judge William Craig, Lord
Craig [89]. The engraver has extended the
body of the sitter to create a three-quarter
length portrait.

Charles Turner 1774–1857 after
Archibald Skirving

150 *Francis Walker Esqr* **1821**

Mezzotint engraving, 30.2 × 25.2cm
(11⁷⁄₈ × 9⁷⁄₈in)
Lettered: *Painted by Mr. Scriven.* [sic] /
Engraved by C. Turner / FRANCIS WALKER ESQR, /
Captain of the 3rd. Troop of East Lothian
Yeomanry Cavalry. / Proof / London,
Published March 1st.. 1821 by C. Turner, 50,
Warren Strt. Fitzroy Square.
Provenance: presented from the Scot Skirving
estate in 1967
Literature: Whitman 1907, p.206, no.588
SCOTTISH NATIONAL PORTRAIT GALLERY

Francis Walker of Tanderlane was a captain in the 3rd Troop East Lothian Yeomanry. The original profile portrait drawing by Skirving is untraced. This print
was made after Skirving's death by one of
the leading mezzotinters in London, who
also engraved many of Raeburn's portraits.

After James Tassie 1735–99

151 *Professor James Robertson*

Plaster medallion, oval, 7.6 (3in) high
Provenance: cast from the original medallion in
the possession of W.G. Patterson in 1889
Literature: Gray 1894, p.140, no.328; Smailes
1990, p.246
SCOTTISH NATIONAL PORTRAIT GALLERY

This plaster cast was made in 1889 from
one of Tassie's original vitreous paste
casts of 1795. An original cast was copied
by Skirving in an untraced drawing (photograph in SNPG archive; fig.23).

The linguist James Robertson (1714–
95) was professor of Hebrew and Oriental
Languages, and librarian, at Edinburgh
University.

Helen Allingham 1848–1926

152 *Thomas Carlyle 1879*

Watercolour, 19.4 × 28cm (7¹¹⁄₁₆ × 11in)
Signed and dated on recto: *H Allingham 1879*
Provenance: purchased in 1915
Literature: Smailes 1990, pp.58–9, ill.
SCOTTISH NATIONAL PORTRAIT GALLERY

Carlyle, the great historian, met Skirving in Edinburgh during 1818. Exactly half a century later he wrote a powerful and affecting memoir of the artist.

George Watson 1767–1837

153 *Archibald Skirving c.1800–10*

Oil on canvas, 73.6 × 60.9cm (29 × 24in)
Provenance: by family descent; Edward Scot Skirving in 1918; Mrs Leila Hoskins; presented to the Haddington Society in 1980; the Lamp of Lothian Trust, Haddington; presented in 1997
Exhibited: RSA, Edinburgh 1918, no.162
Literature: King 1987, p.14, ill.
EAST LOTHIAN COUNCIL MUSEUMS SERVICE

There is a studio copy of this portrait in a private collection, which has also descended collaterally from Archibald Skirving. A differently posed portrait of Skirving by George Watson, and from around the same date, is in the Scottish National Portrait Gallery [154].

George Watson 1767–1837

154 *Archibald Skirving c.1800–10*

Oil on canvas, 90.3 × 69.4cm (35½ × 27¼in)
Provenance: J.K. Watson in 1886; RSA; presented in 1910
Exhibited: Edinburgh 1886, no.1518
Literature: Graves 1913–15, IV, p.1612; Smailes 1990, pp.266–7
SCOTTISH NATIONAL PORTRAIT GALLERY

There is differently posed portrait by Watson of Skirving from around the same date in the collection of the East Lothian Council Museums Service [153]. One of these two portraits was described by a contemporary critic as 'a very strong resemblance of that gentleman; the attitude, as Mr Skirving would say, is *degagée* [free and easy], but there is a remarkable effect of poverty in the colouring, arising perhaps from the dress' (SNPG archive).

After Sir Henry Raeburn 1756–1823

155 *Archibald Skirving c.1810*

[colour plate, back cover]
Oil on canvas, 48.2 × 36.8cm (19 × 14½in)
ANDREW SKIRVING

This is a partial copy after Raeburn's bust-length portrait of Skirving in an American private collection (fig.27), which was retained by Raeburn in his studio as part of his own collection. (Another version of this portrait was offered for sale, but bought in for one guinea, at Christie's, London, 2 July 1831, lot 83, while a later 19th-century copy is in a private collection.) The details of the original are as follows: oil on canvas, 76.2 × 63.5cm (30 × 25in), c.1810; *Provenance:* Sir Henry Raeburn's own collection; John Peter Raeburn of Chesterfield in 1863 and 1867; the Raeburn family in 1876; the Misses Raeburn in 1884; Ralph Cross Johnson; gifted by him in 1919 to the National Gallery of Art, Washington DC, now National Museum of American Art, Smithsonian Institution, Washington DC (no.1919.6.15); de-accessioned at auction, Weschler's, Washington DC, 16 May 1998, lot 41; *Exhibited:* Edinburgh 1863, no.194; Glasgow 1868, no.199; Edinburgh 1876, no.32; Edinburgh 1884, no.372; *Literature:* Armstrong 1901, p.112; Greig 1911, p.59; Mackie 1994.

Andrew Geddes 1783–1844

156 *Captain Robert Skirving of Croys 1813*

Oil on panel, 66 × 45cm (26 × 17½in)
Provenance: the sitter; his son Adam Skirving of Croys; his only child Christina Ainslie Skirving (Mrs Owen Scot Skirving); by family descent to Mrs Leila Hoskins; presented by her in 1981
Literature: NLS, Laing Papers, MS La.IV.26 (Geddes bundle), 'List of Pictures 1813 & 1814', 'no.9 Captain Skirvin [*sic*] (small whole-length)'
SCOTTISH NATIONAL PORTRAIT GALLERY

The sitter was the younger brother of Archibald Skirving, and particularly close to the artist. After a career in the East India Company, Robert returned to farm his estate at Croys in the Stewartry of Kirkcudbright. The painting is in its original frame, and is described in 1818 in the framers' account presented to

Archibald Skirving by William Chalmers & Son of Edinburgh [167]. On 4 April 1818, Chalmers billed Skirving for five shillings for work on an 'an oak frame for a Portrait of his brother by Geddis [*sic*] – and pasting a Board on the face for Backing'. That frame is not the one on the painting, which may be another type referred to on 21 September 1818: 'a Walnut Tree & Gold frame – 9 feet 9 inches at 4/- per foot'. The current frame's construction is common to this period, being mitred with spline inserts – spline meaning a straight or tapered piece of wood inserted into a routed-out groove at right angles to the mitred joint (information kindly provided by Keith Morrison).

Andrew Geddes 1783–1844

157 *Archibald Skirving c.1815–19*

Oil on canvas, 90.3 × 69.4cm (35½ × 27¼in)
Provenance: by family descent to A.A. Scot Skirving Esq; his loan and then bequest to the NGS in 1967; on loan to the SNPG (PGL 313)
Exhibited: Edinburgh 1883, no.40 (lender: R. Scot Skirving Esq); Edinburgh 1901, no.115 (Archibald Scot Skirving)
Literature: Scot Skirving 1988, p.25, ill.; Smailes 1990, pp.266–7, ill; NGS 1997, p.138, ill.
NATIONAL GALLERY OF SCOTLAND

Andrew Geddes copied this portrait of Skirving in etching and drypoint, to which Skirving himself added aquatint [158, fig.28] (Dodgson 1936, pp.36–7, pl.XXIII).

Andrew Geddes 1783–1844 and Archibald Skirving

158 *Archibald Skirving c.1815–19*

[fig.28]
Etching, drypoint and aquatint (6th state), 22 × 15cm (8⅝ × 5⅞in)
Inscribed on recto in pen and ink: *And: Geddes fecit / Aqua forti* [*sic*] *by Mr Skirven* [*sic*] / *Portrait Painter in Pastel*
Provenance: bequeathed by W.F. Watson in 1886
Literature: Dodgson 1936, pp.36–7, pl.XXIII
SCOTTISH NATIONAL PORTRAIT GALLERY

This print is from a series of etchings portraying artists made by Andrew Geddes. According to the very early inscription on this impression, Skirving added the aquatint himself to the etching. It has been copied from Geddes's oil portrait of Skirving [157].

Edward Scriven 1775–1841 after Archibald Skirving

159 ***The Late John Rennie Esqr. c.1821–2***
[fig.26]
Stipple and line engraving, 34 × 27.6cm
(13⅜ × 10⅞in)
Lettered: *S. Kirven* [sic] *delt. / E. Scriven sculp. / THE LATE JOHN RENNIE ESQR. / CIVIL ENGINEER, F. R. S. &c. &c. &c. / Printed by McQueen*
Literature: Walker 1985, I, p.411, II, pl.987
TRUSTEES OF THE NATIONAL PORTRAIT GALLERY, LONDON

The original profile portrait drawing in chalk of the famous engineer (1761–1821), who, like the artist, came from a farming background in East Lothian, is untraced (Cleghorn 1848, II, p.204). That portrait, which was probably drawn in London in 1816, was also engraved in 1862 by W. Holl [162]. In the same year it was included as a focal point in the engraved – and ideal-ised – group portrait, known as *Men of Science in 1807/8* [163–4]. Skirving also appears to have portrayed the sitter's brother, the agriculturist George Rennie of Phantassie, in an untraced three-quar-ter length oil painting (photograph in SNPG archive). George Rennie also ac-quired Skirving's 'keel' portrait drawing of Robert Burns [103] from the studio of the artist, after his death in 1819.

William Walker 1793–1867 after Sir Henry Raeburn 1756–1823

160 ***Sir Henry Raeburn 1826***
Stipple engraving, 27.9 × 23.5cm (11 × 9¼in)
Lettered: *Painted by Himself / Engraved by Willm. Walker / SIR HENRY RAEBURN R.A. / PAINTER TO HIS MAJESTY FOR SCOTLAND, FELLOW OF THE ROYAL SOCIETY &c &c.*
Provenance: bequeathed by W.F. Watson in 1886
Literature: O'Donoghue & Hake 1908–25
SCOTTISH NATIONAL PORTRAIT GALLERY

This stipple engraving by William Walker was published by the engraver in Edin-burgh and London in 1826 and dedicated to George IV. It was based on Raeburn's well-known self-portrait, which belongs to the National Gallery of Scotland (NG 930). Always conscious of his dis-tance from London, Raeburn painted the self-portrait as a diploma piece to im-press a southern audience on his election to the Royal Academy in 1815. As a result the artist's usual bold and easy manner became over-contrived.

William Walker 1793–1867 after Sir Henry Raeburn 1756–1823

161 ***Sir Walter Scott 1826***
Stipple engraving, 27.9 × 23.5cm (11 × 9¼in)
Lettered: *Engraved by Willm. Walker from a Picture by Sir Henry Raeburn R.A. / Walter Scott [facsimile signature] / To the King's most excellent Majesty, / this plate is, (with his gracious permission) humbly Dedicated by His Majesty's most dutiful Subject & Servant, / Willm. Walker / Printed by Mc. Queen / PROOF. / Published 1st. October 1826 by W. Walker No.3. Great King Street Edinburgh, and No. 18, Norton Street, Portland Road, London.*
Literature: O'Donoghue & Hake 1908–25
SCOTTISH NATIONAL PORTRAIT GALLERY

Raeburn's portrait of Scott was com-pleted the year before the artist's death, and this print was published by the en-graver William Walker in the same year as the print of Raeburn's self-portrait [160]. In a letter of 30 May 1816 to Samuel Rogers, the London-based author and critic, Scott praised Skirving's 'keel' portrait drawing of Robert Burns, and the artist as 'a man of great genious [sic] in his art' (Scott 1932–7, IV, pp.243–4).

William Holl 1807–71 after Archibald Skirving

162 ***John Rennie, F.R.S. 1862***
Stipple and line engraving, 29.4 × 20.8cm (11⅝ × 8¼in)
Lettered: *John Rennie, F. R. S. / Engraved by W. Holl after the portrait in Crayons / by Archibald Skirving. / Published by John Murray, Albemarle Street, 1861.*
Literature: Smiles 1862, II, opp. p. 278, ill; Walker 1985, I, p.411
TRUSTEES OF THE NATIONAL PORTRAIT GALLERY, LONDON

This engraving by W. Holl after Skirving's untraced profile portrait drawing of John Rennie was published in 1862 by John Murray in *The Lives of the Engineers* by Samuel Smiles, who described the por-trait as 'on the whole the most lifelike representation of the man as he lived'. Smiles, however, who was only nine when Rennie died, is unlikely to have seen him, or recalled his appearance forty years later if he had.

According to Smiles, the artist and Rennie were close friends, and he noted that the artist 'had as true a genius in him, and might have secured as great a reputation in his own walk, as his friend Rennie, had he worked as patiently and industriously'.

William Walker 1793–1867 and G. Zobel

163 ***The Distinguished Men of Science in Great Britain 1807/8 1862***
Stipple and mezzotint engraving, 63.9 × 108.9cm (24¾ × 42⅞in)
Provenance: William and Elizabeth Walker; their son William Walker; purchased in 1896
Literature: Walker 1985, I, p.605, II, pl.1523
TRUSTEES OF THE NATIONAL PORTRAIT GALLERY, LONDON

Skirving's untraced profile portrait draw-ing of John Rennie was used for the engi-neer's portrait in the centre of this large engraving in which he is shown standing next to the seated figure of James Watt. A key to the engraving was also published [164].

William Walker 1793–1867 and G. Zobel

164 ***Key to the Engraving of the Distinguished Men of Science of Great Britain 1807/8 1862***
Line engraving, 27.3 × 43.5cm (10¾ × 17⅛in)
Provenance: William and Elizabeth Walker; their son William Walker; purchased in 1896
Literature: Walker 1985, I, p.605, II, pl.1524
TRUSTEES OF THE NATIONAL PORTRAIT GALLERY, LONDON

N. Chater & Co. and P. Ronan after Archibald Skirving

165 ***Robert Boswell of St Boswells***
Lithograph, 31.8 × 25.4cm (12½ × 10in)
Lettered: *P. Ronan Del. / N. Chater & Co. Lithog.*
Provenance: Scottish United Services Museum, Edinburgh; presented on permanent loan in 1950
SCOTTISH UNITED SERVICES MUSEUM [ON LOAN TO THE SCOTTISH NATIONAL PORTRAIT GALLERY, EDINBURGH]

This mid-19th-century lithograph is taken from Skirving's pastel portrait of the sitter, drawn c.1795–6 [84]. Robert Boswell (1746–1804), first cousin of James Boswell, the famous biographer of Samuel Johnson, was an Edinburgh lawyer, who was appointed interim Lord Lyon King of Arms for the year 1795–6.

William Holl 1807-71
after Archibald Skirving

166 *Robert Burns*

Lithograph, 47.4 × 33.3cm (18⅝ × 13⅛in)
Lettered: ENGRAVED BY WILLIAM HOLL / ROBERT
BURNS. / From the picture by Archibald Skirving
in the possession of / George Rennie Esqre.
Whitehall, London.
Provenance: purchased in 1884
SCOTTISH NATIONAL PORTRAIT GALLERY

Holl produced this lithograph in the mid-
19th century after Skirving's red chalk
('keel') portrait drawing of Robert Burns
[103], which he had copied from Alexander Nasmyth's oil portrait [51, fig.30].

William Chalmers & Son

167 *Archibald Skirving's Frame
Account 1814-18*

Manuscript
Literature: Houliston 1997, pp.66-8 and 103-4
(Appendix 5)
TRUSTEES OF THE NATIONAL LIBRARY OF
SCOTLAND

The framers were based at 118 High
Street, Edinburgh. The outstanding bill
for £21 15s. was settled by Skirving on 19
December 1818. I am grateful to my colleagues Keith Morrison and Helen
Smailes for their comments on this docu-
ment.

William Bruce

168 *Inventory and Appraisement of
Sundry Effects which belonged to
the late Mr Archibald Skirving 1819*

Manuscript
TRUSTEES OF THE NATIONAL LIBRARY OF
SCOTLAND

William Bruce's valuation of the 'pictures
presumed to be Mr Skirvings Private
Property' was £49 6d. The valuation by
George Watson of the same items was
nearly £900 (see Appendix below).

George Watson 1767-1837

169 *List of Pictures belonging to the
Representatives of the late
Archibald Skirving Esqr. Portrait
Painter 1819*

Manuscript
TRUSTEES OF THE NATIONAL LIBRARY OF
SCOTLAND

The painter George Watson's total valuation of 'Mr Skirvings Paintings' came to
nearly £900, in contrast to William
Bruce's valuation of just under £50 (see
Appendix below).

Attributed to Captain Robert
Skirving of Croys 1757-1843

170 *Epitaphs of Archibald Skirving
(1688-c.1744), Adam Skirving
(1719-1803) and Archibald Skirving
(1749-1819) c.1819*

Printed broadsheet
Provenance: David Laing
UNIVERSITY OF EDINBURGH LIBRARY

These epitaphs of the artist, his father
and grandfather, which are inscribed on
the Skirving family tombstone in the
graveyard of the church at
Athelstaneford, were probably composed by the artist's younger brother,
Robert Skirving [156].

Archibald Skirving

171 *Autograph manuscript of Archibald
Skirving in letter from Adam
Skirving to David Laing 1877*

Manuscript
Provenance: David Laing
UNIVERSITY OF EDINBURGH LIBRARY

The antiquarian David Laing (1793-1878)
amassed papers on Scottish artists,
among which are a series of autograph
notes by and on Skirving.

Captain Robert Skirving of Croys
1757-1843

172 *A Musical Jeu d'Esprit by Archibald
Skirving*

Manuscript
Provenance: David Laing
UNIVERSITY OF EDINBURGH LIBRARY

Throughout his life Archibald Skirving
composed modest pieces of rhyming
verse, a habit which he would have
learned from his father [see 56].

ADDITIONAL ITEMS

Unknown Scottish Artist
after David Martin 1737-98

173 *William Nisbet of Dirleton c.1782*

Watercolour on ivory, oval, 3.8cm (1½in) high
Provenance: by family descent
PRIVATE COLLECTION

William Nisbet of Dirleton (1724-83) was
portrayed by David Martin in an oil portrait
dated 1782 (Private collection). This reduced, miniature copy is by an unknown
Scottish artist, who would have been aware
of Skirving's and Raeburn's works in the
medium. The sitter is shown wearing the
coat of the Caledonian Hunt.

Richard Cosway 1742-1821

174 *Thomas Bruce, 7th Earl of Elgin 1799*

Watercolour on ivory, 7.7cm (3in) high
Signed and dated on verso: *Rd. Cosway R.A./
Primarius / Pictor / Serenissimi / Walliae /
Principis / Pinxit / 1799*
Provenance: by family descent
PRIVATE COLLECTION

Thomas Bruce, 7th Earl of Elgin (1766-1841),
the famous collector of Greek classical sculpture, was portrayed by Cosway in 1799, the
year of his marriage to Mary Hamilton
Nisbet. Another version of this miniature
belongs to the Earl of Elgin and Kincardine
(Edinburgh and London 1995-6, no.180, col.
pl.96). At a time when Skirving was producing miniatures in Edinburgh, many Scottish
sitters chose to be portrayed in this medium
by artists, such as Cosway, who were based in
London.

Attributed to Archibald Skirving

175 *An Unknown Lady c.1780-5*

Watercolour on ivory, 7.7cm (3in) high
Provenance: Daphne Foskett
Literature: Foskett 1987, p.340, col. pl.27A
PRIVATE COLLECTION

This is a characteristic work that can be
attributed to Skirving from the early 1780s.

Attributed to Archibald Skirving

176 *Study of an Unknown Lady's Hands
c.1796-1803*

Pastel, 25.4 × 21.5cm (10 × 8½in)
Provenance: by family descent
ELISABETH A. McINTYRE

This may be 'Lady Dundonnalds [*sic*] hands'
in crayons, which was valued at 8 guineas
(no.31) in George Watson's 1819 valuation of
Skirving's studio contents [169].

BIBLIOGRAPHY

ANDREWS & BROTCHIE 1960
Keith Andrews and James R. Brotchie, *National Gallery of Scotland: Department of Prints and Drawings: Catalogue of Scottish Drawings*, Edinburgh 1960

ARMSTRONG 1901
Sir Walter Armstrong, *Sir Henry Raeburn*, with an Introduction by R.A.M. Stevenson and a Biographical and Descriptive Catalogue by J.L. Caw, London 1901

BAILE DE LAPERRIERE 1991
Charles Baile de Laperriere, *The Royal Scottish Academy Exhibitors 1826–1990*, 4 vols, Calne 1991

BROWN 1995
Iain Gordon Brown, *Elegance & Entertainment in the New Town of Edinburgh: The Harden Drawings*, Edinburgh 1995

BROWN 1996
Iain Gordon Brown, 'The "Real" Pietro Fabris?: A Caricature of Sir William Hamilton's "Favourite Painter"', *Apollo*, CXLIV, no.413, July 1996, pp.39–43

BUCHANAN 1975
David Buchanan, *The Treasure of Auchinleck: The Story of the Boswell Papers*, London 1975

BURLINGTON MAGAZINE 1985
'Recent Museum Acquisitions in Edinburgh', *The Burlington Magazine*, CXXVII, no.989, August 1985, figs.89–102

BURLINGTON MAGAZINE 1997
'Recent Acquisitions in Edinburgh Museums, 1995–97', *The Burlington Magazine*, CXXXIX, no.1133, August 1997, pp.580–4

CARLYLE 1974
Thomas Carlyle, *The Reminiscences of Thomas Carlyle: now first published*, John Clubbe (ed.), Durham (North Carolina) 1974

CAW 1908
James L. Caw, *Scottish Painting Past and Present 1620–1908*, Edinburgh 1908 (repr. 1975)

CHALONER SMITH 1878–84
John Chaloner Smith, *British Mezzotinto Portraits: Being a Descriptive Catalogue of these Engravings from the Introduction of the Art to the early part of the Present Century*, 6 vols, London 1878–83

CLARK 1992
Aylwin Clark, *An Enlightened Scot: Hugh Cleghorn, 1752–1837*, Duns 1992

CLEGHORN 1848
George Cleghorn, *Ancient and Modern Art*, 2nd edn, 2 vols., Edinburgh 1848 (1st edn, 1837)

CLUNE 1966
Frank Clune, *The Scottish Martyrs: The Trials and Transportation to Botany Bay*, Sydney 1969

CULLEN 1984
Fintan Cullen, 'The Oil Paintings of Hugh Douglas Hamilton', *The Walpole Society*, L, 1984, pp.165–208

CUNNINGHAM 1834
Allan Cunningham, *Landscape Illustrations to the Land of Burns*, London 1834

CURSITER 1949
Stanley Cursiter, *Scottish Art to the Close of the Nineteenth Century*, London 1949

DALKEITH HOUSE 1911
H.S. & H.H.D., *Catalogue of the Pictures at Dalkeith House*, privately printed 1911

DODGSON 1934
Campbell Dodgson, *The Etchings of Sir David Wilkie and Andrew Geddes: A Catalogue*, London 1936

DUNCAN 1934
The Revd Thomas O. Duncan, *Athelstaneford: A Poet-haunted Parish in East Lothian*, Edinburgh 1934

ERRINGTON 1988
Lindsay Errington, *David Wilkie 1785–1841* (Scottish Masters Series, no.10), Edinburgh 1988

EVANS & EVANS 1973
Hilary Evans and Mary Evans, *John Kay of Edinburgh: Barber, Miniaturist and Social Commentator 1742–1826*, Aberdeen 1973

FARINGTON 1922–8
Joseph Farington, *The Farington Diary*, 8 vols, London 1922–8

FARINGTON 1978–84
Joseph Farington, *The Diary of Joseph Farington*, Kenneth Garlick, Angus Macintyre and Kathryn Cave (eds), 16 vols, New Haven and London 1978–84 [*Index*, Evelyn Newby (ed.) 1998]

FORD 1981
Brinsley Ford, 'The Grand Tour', *Apollo*, CXIV, December 1981, pp.111–15

FORD 1984
Brinsley Ford, 'The Byres Family by Franciszek Smuglevicz', *National Art-Collections Fund Review*, 1984, pp.111–15

FOSKETT 1972
Daphne Foskett, *A Dictionary of British Miniature Painters*, 2 vols, London 1972

FOSKETT 1974
Daphne Foskett, *John Harden of Brathay Hall 1772–1847*, Kendal 1974

FOSKETT 1987
Daphne Foskett, *Miniatures: Dictionary and Guide*, Woodbridge 1987

FRANKAU 1904
Julia Frankau, *William and James Ward: Their Lives and Works*, London 1904

FREE 1987
Renée Free, *Art Gallery of New South Wales: Catalogue of British Paintings*, Sydney 1987

GARDENSTONE 1802
Lord Gardenstone [Francis Garden], *Travelling Memorandums, made in a Tour upon the Continent of Europe, in the Years 1786, 87, & 88*, 2nd edn, 3 vols, Edinburgh 1802 (1st edn, Edinburgh 1791–5)

GIBSON 1816
Patrick Gibson, *Edinburgh Annual Register 1816* (publ. 1826)

GOLDIE 1975
The Revd George Goldie, 'Parish of Althelstaneford [1792]', Sir John Sinclair (ed.), *Statistical Account of Scotland 1791–1799*, repr. Wakefield 1975

GORDON 1951
T. Crouther Gordon, *David Allan of Alloa 1744–1796: The Scottish Hogarth*, Alva 1951

GOW 1996
Ian Gow, 'The Dining Room', *The Scottish Home*, Annette Carruthers (ed.), Edinburgh 1996, pp.126–54

GRAVES 1905–6
Algernon Graves, *The Royal Academy of Arts: A Complete Dictionary of Contributors and their work from its foundation in 1769 to 1904*, 8 vols, London 1905–6

GRAVES 1913–15
Algernon Graves, *A Century of Loan Exhibitions 1813–1912*, 5 vols, London 1913–15

GRAY 1894
John M. Gray, *James and William Tassie: A Biographical and Critical Sketch with a Catalogue of their Portrait Medallions of Modern Personages*, Edinburgh 1894

GRAY & JAMIESON 1941
W. Forbes Gray and James H. Jamieson, *East Lothian Biographies*, Haddington 1941

GREIG 1911
James Greig, *Sir Henry Raeburn, R.A.: His Life and Works with a Catalogue of his Pictures*, London 1911

HERD 1973
David Herd (ed.), *Ancient and Modern Scottish Songs, Heroic Ballads, &c*, 2 vols, Edinburgh and London 1973 (1st edn, 2 vols, Edinburgh 1776)

HOGG 1821
James Hogg (ed.), *The Jacobite Relics of Scotland; being the Songs, Airs and Legends, of the Adherents to the House of Stuart*, Edinburgh 1821 [58]

HOLLOWAY 1986
James Holloway, *James Tassie 1735–1799* (Scottish Masters Series, no.1), Edinburgh 1986

HOLLOWAY 1987
James Holloway, *Jacob More 1740–1793* (Scottish Masters Series, no.4), Edinburgh 1987

HOULISTON 1997
Laura R. Houliston, 'Framemaking in Edinburgh 1790–1830', unpublished M.Phil. Thesis, University of Glasgow 1997

INGAMELLS 1997
John Ingamells, *A Dictionary of British and Irish Travellers in Italy 1701–1800: Compiled from the Brinsley Ford Archive*, London 1997

IRWIN 1973
Francina Irwin, 'Early Raeburn Reconsidered', *The Burlington Magazine*, CXV, no.841, April 1973, pp.239–44

IRWIN & IRWIN 1975
David Irwin and Francina Irwin, *Scottish Painters at Home and Abroad 1700–1900*, London 1975

JOHNSON & STENHOUSE 1853
James Johnson and William Stenhouse, *The Scots Musical Museum*, 4 vols, Edinburgh and London 1853

KING 1987
Moyra King, *Athelstaneford*, Bonnyrigg 1987

LAING 1914–25
Historical Manuscripts Commission: Report on the Laing Manuscripts Preserved in the University of Edinburgh, 2 vols, London 1914–25

LAING 1974
Alistair Laing, 'Through English Eyes', *Country Life*, CLVI, no.402, 8 August 1974, p.348

LANDRETH 1933
P.R. Landreth, 'Burns's Portraits: the Skirving Sketch', *The Scotsman*, 12 September 1933

LLOYD WILLIAMS 1994
Julia Lloyd Williams, *Gavin Hamilton 1723–1798* (Scottish Masters Series, no.18), Edinburgh 1994

LOCHE & ROETHLISBERGER 1978
Renée Loche and Marcel Roethlisberger, *L'Opera Completa di Liotard*, Milan 1978

MCINTYRE & MCKIRDY 1997
Donald B. McIntyre and Alan McKirdy, *James Hutton: The Founder of Modern Geology*, Edinburgh 1997

MACKENZIE 1927
Henry Mackenzie, *The Anecdotes and Egotisms of Henry Mackenzie 1745–1831: now first published*, Harold William Thompson (ed.), London 1927

MACKENZIE-STUART 1995
A.J. Mackenzie-Stuart, *A French King at Holyrood*, Edinburgh 1995

MACKIE 1994
David Mackie, 'Raeburn: Life and Art', unpublished Ph.D. Thesis, 6 vols, University of Edinburgh, 1994

MACMILLAN 1990
Duncan Macmillan, *Scottish Art 1460–1990*, Edinburgh 1990

MANNERS 1932
Lady Victoria Manners, 'Catherine Read and Royal Patronage', *The Connoisseur*, LXXXII, January 1932, pp.35–40

MILNER 1997
Catherine Milner, 'Earliest Portraits by Raeburn Discovered', *The Sunday Telegraph*, 23 November 1997, p.7

MONTAIGLON AND GUIFFREY 1887–1912
Correspondance des Directeurs de l'Académie de France à Rome avec les Surintendants des Bâtiments, A. De Montaiglon and J. Guiffrey (eds), 16 vols, Paris 1887–1912

NACF *REVIEW* 1995
National Art Collections Fund Review, London 1995

NACF *REVIEW* 1996
National Art Collections Fund Review, London 1996

NAEF 1956
Hans Naef, 'Ingres' Portrait Drawings of English Sitters in Rome', XCVIII, no.645, December 1956, pp.427–35

NAEF 1977–80
Hans Naef, *Die Bildniszeichnungen von J.-A.-D. Ingres*, 5 vols, Berne 1977–80

NGS 1980
National Gallery of Scotland: Illustrations, Edinburgh 1980

NGS 1997
The National Gallery of Scotland: Concise Catalogue of Paintings, Edinburgh 1997

NICHOLAS 1973
Donald Nicholas, *The Portraits of Bonnie Prince Charlie*, Maidstone 1973

NOON 1981
John Murdoch, Jim Murrell, Patrick J. Noon and Roy Strong, *The English Miniature*, New Haven and London 1981, pp.163–209

O'DONOGHUE & HAKE 1908–25
Freeman O'Donoghue and Henry M. Hake, *Catalogue of the Engraved British Portraits preserved in the Department of Prints and Drawings in the British Museum*, 6 vols, 1908–25

OMOND 1887
George W.T. Omond, *The Arniston Memoirs: Three Centuries of a Scottish House 1571–1838: edited from the family papers*, Edinburgh 1887

PORTALIS 1910
Baron Roger Portalis, *Henri-Pierre Danloux: Peintre de Portraits et son Journal durant l'Emigration (1753–1809)*, Paris 1910

REYNOLDS 1988
Graham Reynolds, *English Portrait Miniatures*, Cambridge 1988 (1st edn, 1952)

RUSSELL 1777
John Russell, *Elements of Painting with Crayons*, 2nd edn, London 1777

SCOT SKIRVING 1988
Memoirs of Dr Robert Scot Skirving 1859–1956, Ann Macintosh (ed.), Sydney 1988

SCOTS MAGAZINE
[Review of Exhibition of Society of Artists], *The Scots Magazine*, 1812, p.247

SCOTT 1932–7
The Letters of Sir Walter Scott, H.J.C. Grierson (ed.), 12 vols, London 1932–7

SIMON 1987
Robin Simon, *The Portrait in Britain and America: with a Biographical Dictionary of Portrait Painters*, Oxford 1987

SKINNER 1959
Basil C. Skinner, 'A "Keel" head of Burns', *Scotland's Magazine*, January 1959, pp.43–4

SKINNER 1963
Basil C. Skinner, *Burns: Authentic Likenesses*, Edinburgh 1963

SKINNER 1970
Basil C. Skinner, 'Archibald Skirving and his Work', *Transactions of the East Lothian Antiquarian and Field Naturalists' Society*, XII, 1970, pp.46–56

SKINNER 1990
Basil C. Skinner, *Burns: Authentic Likenesses*, Darvel 1990

SKIRVING 1794
The Trial of William Skirving, Edinburgh 1794

SKIRVING 1836
The Trial of William Skirving; ... with an Original Memoir, and Notes, Glasgow 1836

SMAILES 1990
Helen Smailes, *The Concise Catalogue of the Scottish National Portrait Gallery*, Edinburgh 1990

SMAILES 1992
Helen Smailes, *Kenneth Macleay 1802–1878* (Scottish Masters Series, no.16), Edinburgh 1992

SMILES 1862
Samuel Smiles, *The Lives of the Engineers with an Account of their Principal Works; Comprising also a History of Inland Communication in Britain*, 2 vols, London 1862

SPROTT 1996
Gavin Sprott, *Robert Burns: Pride and Passion: The Life, Times and Legacy*, Edinburgh 1996

STEUART 1890
A. Francis Steuart, *Catalogue of the Pictures at Dalkeith House*, Dalkeith 1890

SUNDSTRÖM 1994
Tanja Sundström, *Aspects of the Life and Work of Archibald Skirving (1749–1819)*, unpublished M.Phil. Thesis, University of St Andrews 1994

TANCRED 1903
George Tancred of Weens, *Annals of a Border Club (The Jedforest) and Biographical Notices of the Families Contained therewith*, 2nd edn, Edinburgh 1903 (1st edn, 1899)

THOMSON 1994
Duncan Thomson, *Sir Henry Raeburn 1756–1823* (Scottish Masters Series, no.21), Edinburgh 1994

WALKER 1985
Richard Walker, *Regency Portraits in the National Portrait Gallery*, 2 vols, London 1985

WALPOLE SOCIETY 1998
'The Ford Collection', *Walpole Society*, 2 vols, LX, 1998

WATERHOUSE 1981
Ellis Waterhouse, *The Dictionary of British 18th Century Painters in Oils and Crayons*, Woodbridge 1981

WHITMAN 1903
Alfred Whitman, *Nineteenth Century Mezzotinters: Samuel William Reynolds*, London 1903

WHITMAN 1907
Alfred Whitman, *Nineteenth Century Mezzotinters: Charles Turner*, London 1907

ZACHS 1998
William Zachs, *The First John Murray and the late Eighteenth-century London Book Trade, with a Checklist of his Publications*, Oxford 1998

Exhibition Catalogues

BONN 1993
Sehsucht: Das Panorama als Massenunterhaltung des 19. Jahrhunderts, Kunst und Ausstellungshalle der Bundesrepublik Deutschland, Bonn 1993

EDINBURGH 1810
Associated Society of Artists, Edinburgh 1810

EDINBURGH 1812
The Society of Artists, York Place [Raeburn's Studio], Edinburgh 1812

EDINBURGH 1863
Works of Deceased and Living Scottish Artists, Royal Scottish Academy, Edinburgh 1863

EDINBURGH 1876
Sir Henry Raeburn, R.A., Royal [Scottish] Academy & National Galleries [of Scotland], Edinburgh 1876

EDINBURGH 1883
Works of Old Masters & Scottish National Portraits, Board of Manufactures, Edinburgh 1883

EDINBURGH 1884
Scottish National Portraits, Board of Manufactures, Edinburgh 1884

EDINBURGH 1901
Pictures by Sir Henry Raeburn and other Deceased Painters of the Scottish School, National Gallery of Scotland, Edinburgh 1901

EDINBURGH 1951
Scotland Yet: Exhibition of Historic Scottish Treasures, Moubray House, Edinburgh 1951

EDINBURGH 1955
Portrait Drawings by Scottish Artists 1750–1850, Scottish National Portrait Gallery, Edinburgh 1955

EDINBURGH 1965
British Portrait Miniatures, Daphne Foskett (ed.), The Arts Council Gallery, Rothesay Terrace, Edinburgh 1965

EDINBURGH 1966
Scots in Italy in the 18th Century, [Basil C. Skinner (ed.)], Scottish National Portrait Gallery, Edinburgh 1966

EDINBURGH 1976
A Face for Any Occasion: Some Aspects of Portrait Engraving, Sara Stevenson (ed.), Scottish National Portrait Gallery, Edinburgh 1976

EDINBURGH 1981
Masterpieces of Scottish Portraiture, Duncan Macmillan (ed.), Talbot Rice Art Centre, The University of Edinburgh 1981

EDINBURGH 1985
A French Painter in Exile: Henri-Pierre Danloux (1753–1809), Helen Smailes (ed.), Scottish National Portrait Gallery, Edinburgh 1985 [part of the publication *France in the National Galleries of Scotland*]

EDINBURGH 1990
Scotland's Pictures, Royal Scottish Academy, Edinburgh 1990

EDINBURGH 1993
The Line of Tradition: Watercolours, Drawings & Prints by Scottish Artists 1700–1990, Mungo Campbell (ed.), Royal Scottish Academy, Edinburgh 1993

EDINBURGH 1995
The Three Graces: Antonio Canova, Aidan Weston-Lewis (ed.), National Gallery of Scotland, Edinburgh 1995

EDINBURGH 1996
Christina Roberston: A Scottish Portraitist at the Russian Court, City Art Centre, Edinburgh 1996

EDINBURGH 1996–7
Portrait Miniatures from the Collection of the Duke of Buccleuch, Stephen Lloyd (ed.), Scottish National Portrait Gallery, Edinburgh 1996–7

EDINBURGH AND KILMARNOCK 1996
Robert Burns: Pride and Passion: The Life, Times and Legacy, Royal Museum of Scotland, Edinburgh and the Dick Institute, Kilmarnock 1996

EDINBURGH AND LONDON 1967
Mr Boswell, John Kerslake (ed.), Scottish National Portrait Gallery, Edinburgh and National Portrait Gallery, London 1967

EDINBURGH AND LONDON 1986–7
Painting in Scotland: The Golden Age, Duncan Macmillan (ed.), Talbot Rice Art Centre, University of Edinburgh and Tate Gallery, London 1986–7

EDINBURGH AND LONDON 1995–6
Richard & Maria Cosway: Regency Artists of Taste and Fashion, Stephen Lloyd (ed.), Scottish National Portrait Gallery, Edinburgh and National Portrait Gallery, London 1995–6

EDINBURGH AND LONDON 1997–8
Raeburn: The Art of Sir Henry Raeburn 1756–1823, Duncan Thomson (ed.), Royal Scottish Academy, Edinburgh and National Portrait Gallery, London, 1997–8

FLORENCE AND SPOLETO 1988
Le Peintre François-Xavier Fabre, Laure Pellicer (ed.), Galleria degli Uffizi and Palazzo Raconi-Arroni, Spoleto 1988

GENEVA AND PARIS 1992
Dessins de Liotard: Suivi du Catalogue de l'oeuvre dessiné, Anne de Herdt (ed.), Musée d'art et d'histoire, Geneva and Musée du Louvre, Paris 1992

GLASGOW 1868
Portraits, Corporation Buildings, Glasgow 1868

LIVERPOOL 1994–5
Face to Face: Three Centuries of Artists' Self-Portraiture, Xanthe Brooke (ed.), Walker Art Gallery, Liverpool 1994–5

LONDON 1865
Portrait Miniatures, South Kensington Museum, London 1865

LONDON 1939
Scottish Art, Royal Academy of Arts, London 1939

LONDON 1956–7
British Portraits, Royal Academy of Arts, London 1956–7

LONDON 1968
Englishmen in Italy, Victoria & Albert Museum, London 1968

LONDON 1974
British Artists in Rome 1700–1800, Lindsay Stainton (ed.), The Iveagh Bequest, Kenwood, London 1974

LONDON 1996
Vases & Volcanoes: Sir William Hamilton and his Collection, Ian Jenkins and Kim Sloan (eds), British Museum, London 1996

LONDON 1996–7
The Art of the Picture Frame: Artists, Patrons and the Framing of Portraits in Britain, Jacob Simon (ed.), National Portrait Gallery, London 1996–7

LONDON AND ROME 1996–7
Grand Tour: The Lure of Italy in the Eighteenth Century, Ilaria Bignamini and Andrew Wilton (eds), Tate Gallery, London and Palazzo delle Esposizioni, Rome 1996–7

LONDON 1998
John Murray I, William Zachs (ed.), British Academy, London 1998

NORWICH 1958
Eighteenth-Century Italy and the Grand Tour, Castle Museum, Norwich 1958

PAISLEY AND EDINBURGH 1977
John Henning 1771–1851, Paisley Art Gallery and Scottish National Portrait Gallery, Edinburgh 1977

ROME 1959
Il Settecento a Roma, Palazzo delle Esposizioni, Rome 1959

SHEFFIELD 1952
Drawings from the Collection of Mr Paul Oppé, Graves Art Gallery, Sheffield 1952

SYDNEY 1981
Scottish Paintings from the Collection: Art Gallery of New South Wales, Renée Free (ed.), Art Gallery of New South Wales, Sydney 1981

APPENDIX
SKIRVING'S STUDIO CONTENTS IN 1819

Skirving's studio contents included numerous portfolios of drawings and prints, as well as just under forty glazed and framed portraits and other subjects, which either had been retained by the artist for personal reasons, or because they were unfinished, had not been paid for or were unclaimed by the sitters. The value of the contents had initially been estimated by a professional valuer, William Bruce, at just under fifty pounds. When revalued by the portraitist George Watson, a more realistic valuation of nearly one thousand pounds was arrived at.

The most expensive single item was the pastel head of *Gavin Hamilton* [60], valued by Watson at 100 guineas. This was followed by finished drawings of a *Venus and Cupid* (80 guineas) and of a *Grecian Statue* (50 guineas). Of the other more expensively valued pastel portraits, there was a lady in black, *Mary Graham* of Glasgow (50 guineas), as well as the unfinished portrait of *Lady Charlotte Campbell* [98, fig.18] and the finished head of her husband *Colonel John Campbell of Shawfield*, valued at £106 4s. for the pair, a figure which included seventeen years' interest. The incomplete portrait of *Maria Cuninghame of Lainshaw* [100, fig.19] was valued at £35, while the unfinished 'keel' portrait drawing of *Robert Burns* after Nasmyth [103] was valued at the surprisingly modest figure of £30 10s. The drawing after Delacour of the seal engraver *William Berry* [105] was estimated at 20 guineas. The pastel of the artist's half-sister *Janet Skirving, Mrs James Carnegie of Edrom Newton* [85] and his *Self-portrait* [61] drawn in Rome in 1790 also appear but are unvalued. Other identifiable portraits are listed in the valuation, including the head of *Professor Dugald Stewart* [115], which was probably started by John Henning and completed by Skirving (20 guineas); the 'full-length Painting of a[n] Architect supposed Craig supposed by D Allan' [47, fig.8], valued at £26 5s.; 'Lady Dundonnalds hands' in crayons (5 guineas) [176]; and *Captain Walker* [150] (30 guineas).

Despite having a collection of prints, Skirving owned very few paintings by other artists. Apart from the portrait of *Professor Dugald Stewart* started by Henning and completed by Skirving, and that of *James Craig* ascribed to David Allan, Skirving owned a framed and glazed portrait 'of a French painter by a Lady' – valued by Watson at 8 guineas – and a painting of a horse by James Howe (1780–1836), valued by Bruce at 2s.6d. It is also known that Skirving owned a small oil on copper painting by the Austrian landscape painter Franz de Paula Ferg (1689–1740), who had moved to London in 1724. This painting was described as 'a landscape with figure, a group near a fountain, among them is a man holding a spirited horse, a romantic distance'. This was in the 1807 auction of the collection of pictures belonging to the landscapist George Walker. In the latter's own descriptive catalogue, he noted that the painting formerly 'belonged to the ingenious Mr. Skirving, well known for his excellent Portraits in Crayon; and who, on going many years since to Italy to prosecute his studies, parted with it to a friend'.

Among the portfolios were portraits in coloured crayons, including five heads and a pair of hands (£10); 45 portraits in black and red chalk (2 guineas); 63 drawings and prints, chiefly academy figures (15 guineas); and 112 drawings and prints of various subjects (£5 12s.). There were also portfolios of prints: 26 modern portrait prints (£5 4s.); 19 Italian landscape prints (£2 7s.3d.); 411 miscellaneous prints (£10); and a book of etchings after Salvator Rosa (3 guineas). William Bruce also noted two miniatures, presumably by Skirving, of unknown gentlemen (10s.6d.). Among other items left by Skirving in his studio, Bruce noted twelve drawing books (5s.) and a box containing a few books and pamphlets (10s.), but only one itemised book (7s.6d.). This was a copy of *The Art of Painting*, an English edition of the classic 17th-century poem *De arte grafica*, by the French painter and art critic Charles Alphonse Du Fresnoy, which went through numerous translations across Europe in the 18th century.

Bruce also listed a few pieces of mahogany furniture: a cabinet (3 guineas), a drawing table (2 guineas), a small writing table with two drawers containing drawing materials (15s.), a desk (7s.6d.), a firescreen (2s.6d.) and a small stand (2s.). Finally, the valuer listed various miscellaneous items for drawing, including small cases with crayons (1 guinea) and a plate of glass for grinding colours. Among the sundries were a gold thimble, a cornelian seal, some sleeve buttons, a small silver tea ladle and some hair pencils (12s.6d.); a parcel of bone egg spoons and egg cups with some iron screws and nails (5s.); and a very small quantity of gentlemen's 'wearing apparel' (£3 7s.6d.), as well as an old silver watch (£4 5s.).

INDEX OF ARTISTS

INDEX OF SITTERS